Tales from The Tap Room

Steve Morley was born in Yorkshire, the first son of a window-cleaner and school-dinner lady. On leaving school he became a vegetable porter, then a scrap-metal worker and a trainee teacher. He reluctantly abandoned teaching to become a champion chicken slaughterer for which he was given the nickname of 'Claudius' because 'he murdered most foul'.

After a short spell in uniform (for Bradford City Transport) he left for the bright smoke of London to pursue a career as an actor. Stage and TV appearances followed; he played a crazed blinder of horses, a spotty neurotic, a child kidnapper, many a drunkard and a space-invader machine operator pitted against the Cybermen.

Many other roles were similarly typecast.

He now lives in a bedsit, which he regards as cooking in the office and sleeping in the kitchen. He is not married, has no children to his knowledge but has a perfect on-going relationship with a spider-plant called Gertrude.

Tales from
The Tap Room

STEVE MORLEY

with a foreword by
Colin Milburn

A METHUEN PAPERBACK

*First published in Great Britain in 1986
by Methuen London Ltd
11 New Fetter Lane, London EC4P 4EE*

*Text Copyright © 1986 by Steve Morley
Illustrations © 1986 by Methuen London Ltd
Cover design and illustrations by Paul Davies*

Made and printed in Great Britain

British Library Cataloguing in Publication Data

Morley, Steve
   Tales from the tap room.
   1. Cricket – Anecdotes, facetiae, satire,
   etc.
   I. Title
   796.35'8'0207   GV919

   ISBN0-413-14570-0

to Mam and Grandma for everything,
and to Abbi for listening

Contents

ACKNOWLEDGEMENTS

Thanks to Colin Milburn for paying his round; to Leon Griffiths for the champagne; to Matthew Engels for his advice at closing time; to Tony 'Fingers' Ashton for his advice at opening time; and to all at the Ferret and Firkin Tap Room. And special thanks to Roger Fox whose memory for the oldest and worst of jokes made much of this book possible.

Foreword

When I was asked to write a foreword to *Tales From The Tap Room* I was delighted to accept for two reasons. Firstly because it involves cricket and secondly because it involves my other favourite love, apart from sport: public houses.

Over the years playing cricket at most levels has made me realise that cricket and pubs go together wherever you are playing, from the West Indies to Australia.

In fact, when I used to play county cricket if the ground on which we were playing didn't have a players' bar, after each day's play we headed for the nearest pub with the opposition to discuss the game over a pint. Even the captain was given expenses to buy his team and the opposition the first round. The opposition captain did the same, so we were given the first two rounds – which satisfied some of the more careful players in the side! (Note that we were only allowed to have beer at that stage in the evening!)

Drink also had that numbing effect, which was great if you got hit by the ball.

I remember one occasion in Perth, Western Australia, when I was playing for WA against the visiting West Indians. Our captain was Tony Lock, former Surrey and England left-arm spinner. He came on to bowl with five minutes to go on the Saturday evening and immediately asked me to field at forward short leg – but very close. The batsman was West Indian opener Joey Carew, who was also left-handed.

The first ball was a long hop which Joey pulled straight into my face (no helmets in those days) and hit me on the cheekbone. I went down like a sack of bricks but picked myself up and finished the over, which was the last of the day.

The doctor was convinced that I had fractured my cheekbone but couldn't do anything about it. I was in a lot of pain but went with the players to the Trots, a form of racing with horses and buggies, where I was provided with a large supply of whisky by sympathetic supporters. This helped ease the pain and that night I slept like a lamb.

I told Tony Lock the next day that I wasn't up to fielding because of my sore cheekbone. In fact the real reason was because of my bad head which was due to a very heavy hangover. If Lockie reads this book he'll know the truth.

There have been many occasions at both Test and county level where players have probably consumed too much the night before and have taken the field not at their best. In fact, when you next watch a Test or county match and you see the batsmen talking at the end of the over, you may assume that they are discussing the state of the wicket or the standard of the bowling; but it is more than likely that they are discussing the state of each other's health after the night before.

This is a very funny book and as I know a few of the boys personally I can assure everyone that they enjoy both their cricket and their beer. I sincerely hope that people who read this book get as much pleasure as I did from it.

1· *The Old Team Photograph*

2 September 1985

Dear Lucky,

How are you, you old 'Chinaman' you? It's been a long time, eh mate? So here's greetings from a soaking South Hampstead – everyone sends their regards and best wishes from the Ferret and Firkin.

All the old crowd are still there: the same old faces, the same old complaints – usually these days about Australian lager. I mean, why they should want to send it over here along with their bar staff and rucksacks is beyond me. And all those girlfriends with names that sound like man-made fibres – you know – Rayleen and Shirleen and the like. (Dave the Grave went over there on a holiday recently and when he got off the plane they asked him if he had a criminal record. He apologised and said he didn't realise that it was still compulsory.)

And did you see those two advertising hoardings above the Tavern at Lord's this summer when the One-day International was on? There was the usual one for Fosters lager and alongside it, in almost exactly the same lettering and colours, was another saying 'People Prefer Gas'. Nice to know that someone in the Long Room still has a sense of humour.

Anyway Lucky, the reason I'm writing is this: first of all, everyone is so happy that the operation went so well and we're looking forward to seeing you again. We intend to throw a little party for you at the Ferret, so let us know when you'll be back. (Actually, we need another good excuse for an extension.)

...CRACK'
CRONIN THE LIBRARIAN

But more importantly, do you remember that cricket team you formed at the Ferret all those years ago – the one that ended up with that unfortunate punch-up between the not-very-accurate fast bowler and the square leg umpire? I'm sure you do. Didn't you retire after that game? And maybe it's just a rumour, but I heard that you burned all your kit afterwards and still keep the ashes in a Golden Delicious box in your shed; but you know what pubs are like for rumours – especially the Ferret and Firkin.

Well, some months ago the new landlord was having a spring clean and he came across the team photograph, and by the Lord Harry we had a good laugh! Everyone looked so young and you look so much better without the goitre. And I don't know, Lucky, but I think it's a shame if you did burn all your kit as I'm sure that flared whites will come back in some day.

I'm afraid I didn't recognise all the people in the picture, but there were a few faces that are still knocking 'em back at the Ferret.

There was good old Robin the Hood. It was the first time I'd seen him without that special coat he always wore to go shopping in – and doesn't he look slim? (I don't know if you've heard about Robin, but he's presently doing three years in the Scrubs after being found in possession of sixty Millwall FC strips. I can't imagine who in their right minds would have bought any of them from him, but after all the football troubles this year the court thought it had to make an example.)

Then, standing next to you with that permanent Neolithic grin is a young Arthur Cronin. He's still around: still chewing the odd pint mug when the pub runs out of scratchings. He's now working for Camden Libraries as a bouncer. We've nicknamed him Cronin the Librarian. Didn't he once run down the wicket to a very short-pitched off-break, when he missed the ball completely and was clean bowled, although his bat went for six?

In the back row there's all six foot eleven of Dave the Grave. Well, I presume it's him because unfortunately the photographer cut off most of his head, which is hardly surprising really. But if, like me, you've been watching the recent re-runs of *The Addams Family*, then there's no mistaking the Lurch-like figure of Dave. I'm told that he made an absolutely appalling first slip because by the time his brain had sent the message to his hands the ball was dancing merrily away for four.

Next to him is our old friend Fingers Ashton, the pub pianist, wearing the most outrageous wicket-keeping gloves I've ever seen. It's not clear, but it looks as though he's balancing two pints of ale on one thumb. I know that everyone has a living to make to subsidise their cricket-playing but those gloves make me wonder if the team had any insurance at all. Maybe you will enlighten me, but they look very much like a pair of baseball catcher's mits – both left-handed at that. I can't understand why Fingers has the reputation of never being able to hold anything except a pint glass: with those gloves you could catch Exocets!

At the front of the picture there was what at first glimpse I took to be a very nice touch indeed. By the Lord Neddy, I thought, they had a club mascot just like all those army regiments – though this one looked more like the black pig that Nelson had at Trafalgar, and it was dressed in its whites. But on closer inspection I realised that it was little Dick Dickinson, the West Indian all-rounder. And pretty all-round he looks too. I thought that years of serious drinking had gone into that shape of his but he appears to have been born with it. And, by the Lord Joel, he had curly hair! You know, the usual West Indian stuff. Since he came back from his four-year holiday to Jamaica, where he was sorting out his tax affairs, he's had his hair straightened. I mean it! Brylcreem and all. He now looks like a dwarfish cross between Viv Richards and Fred Trueman. He still has the same expression on his face – like the man whose finger has just gone through the toilet paper.

As I say, there were many others there that I failed to recognise. Especially the two women, who I presume were the two tea-ladies; but by the Lord Betsy they were better turned out than anyone else. I've never seen a more diversely turned out cricket side. It could easily have been a Lillywhites catalogue picture of jumpers and caps.

But there was one touch which I found quite exciting, as I knew the picture was taken long before the days when all Test batsmen wore protective headgear. The man wearing the Lambretta crash helmet was years ahead of his time and I'm thinking seriously of sending a copy of this picture to Lord's, as documentary evidence of how the humble pub cricketer has had a definite influence on the game right up to international level.

And some of those whites! If they can be called whites – the degree of whiteness varied from leg to leg, from kneecap to ankle even. Some of those whites could have been family heirlooms. The man wearing the pair of thirty-five-inch bottoms and turn-ups must have been positively dangerous once the wind got up. But Lucky, and I hope you don't mind me saying this, I should try to get hold of a pair like those for yourself. They look just the thing for disguising a colostomy.

And the pads! By the Lord Knotty, I didn't know individual designer pads existed in those days – or am I showing my ignorance? Some of them had definitely seen better days; and the chap who's tied his on with bits of washing-line looks like a Morris dancer who'd wandered into the picture.

I don't know how typical this picture is of your usual pub cricket team, Lucky, but it certainly caused quite a stir down at the Ferret and Firkin, I can tell you. So much so, and I know you'll be pleased to hear this, that enough of us were spurred into re-forming the side. Yes! The Ferret and Firkin CC lives again. We've already played out most of our first season and I'll tell you more about that later. Needless to say, it has been very eventful.

All of this came about thanks to the organisational skill of a new customer whom I don't believe you have met. He's a Mr Gloomburg, who used to make a living inventing new drinks – and I must say that we have a grand time if he's around and there's an extension, doing bits of market research, you know. He now advises various companies on brand names etc. and was instrumental in stopping an American frozen fish company from introducing a new brand called 'Tasty Cod Pieces'. We're all very grateful to him.

So, the Ferret and Firkin CC is now affiliated to the CCC, the AMCC, the NCA and the National Association of Advertising Practitioners for all I know.

We organised various events, such as raffles, yard of ale competitions, guessing what the hell was in one of Mr Gloomburg's latest concoctions and so forth in order to raise funds. All of which led to that great day when we bought the first piece of equipment for the club – the team jug. It was duly christened, or rather it was christened Julie after a rather attractive barmaid whom we now have the pleasure of ogling.

As I say, Lucky, I'll let you know more in due course.

Hope you are not in too much pain. Always remember Jasper Vinall who, in 1624, at Horsted Keynes in Sussex, was killed while he was, quite rightly, preventing an opponent from having two hits at the ball.

With regards,

Steve.

2· *Reforming the Side*

15 October 1985

Dear Lucky,

I was so sorry to hear that the same day you received my last letter you had a relapse.

It has often been mooted around the Ferret and Firkin that surgeons should take advanced courses in needlecraft – well, at least a City and Guilds'. As you know, we have many a medical type of person amongst our company, and when the matter of your stitches was discussed it was generally agreed that your surgeon had been practising his crochet technique. Anyway, enclosed is a nice pattern that someone cut out of *Woman's Own*. Let's hope that the next fellow makes a better job of it.

All of which reminds me of a game we were playing last season and we had two medical wallahs batting. It was most strange.

At one end there was Sean Kildare, your old friend the Irish gynaecologist (didn't he once decorate your house through the letter-box?), and at the other there was Dr Richard Payne, the local National Health GP (he's recently gone into partnership with Dr William Hurt).

We were all sitting in the pavilion, or to be more accurate on a couple of park benches under an oak tree, and all of a sudden everybody just left the field – fielders, umpires, batsmen, the lot. They just ran away.

It was most extraordinary. It was as if they were all chasing the same ball as they disappeared into the housing estate beyond – you must know the one: it's festooned with GLC barrage balloons. After about twenty minutes they all returned, all grins and social chit-chat.

17

Well, you can imagine the speculation in the 'pavilion'. We all thought that someone had discovered a pub serving after hours. What else could have been responsible for such an exodus?

What happened was actually quite straightforward.

A local born-again Mormon milkman had had a nasty accident with several bottles of Gold Top. His screams were heard by the players, who thought that a young girl was being molested, and off they went, a host of knight errants, to save the damsel in distress.

Fortunately, the gynaecologist was first to arrive. The milkman, who was in a state of shock, upon seeing the padded-up gynaecologist closely followed by fourteen other similarly clad saviours, thought it was the Messiah batting for England. He promptly crossed himself and passed out. The gynaecologist, after surveying the poor unfortunate's injuries, promptly referred the case over to the GP.

Who says that pub cricket teams are unprofessional?

Anyway Lucky, you poor little off-break you, you may remember me telling you about our advertising-consultant friend Mr Gloomburg. Well, it was he who was responsible for getting the new Ferret and Firkin CC together.

He's an amazing man. We were selling Ferret and Firkin CC souvenir sweatbands and bookmarks long before we had any fixtures! But of course, we had to raise funds.

Our raffle was quite astonishing. The new landlord donated a first prize of a gallon of Australian lager and a second prize of two gallons.

Mr Gloomburg donated a beautifully framed advertisement. This was one that got away from him and you may remember it. Some years ago the West Yorkshire police force were doing a recruitment drive to attract more women into the force – not a bad idea at that. On the left was a picture of a policeman and next to him, slightly lower down, was a policewoman. Alongside were these words:

Q. What is the difference between a policewoman and a policeman?
A. Six inches.

(By the Lord Peel I bet that stirred them up in the Bradford League; and I couldn't help thinking of it when that bemused young plodder took tea on the Headingley Test Match pitch this year.)

There were also several prizes of reproduction urns of the Ashes. A gross in fact – if your number came up you won a dozen of them. These were donated by Robin the Hood from his bedsit in B-Wing of the Scrubs; and by the Lord Turpin did you see David Gower being presented with one by Peter West after the Oval Test? I'm sure it was one of the same lot. If we could have had a close-up of the bottom of it you'd have been able to read, 'Made in Taiwan'.

We also made quite a bit of money on a book run by Dick Dickinson, the Brylcreemed West Indian, on a knockout darts match. This was marred slightly by Cronin the Librarian who threw three darts with a googly action. The safest place in the pub to stand was with your nose right in front of the treble twenty.

As soon as all the money was gathered, the pace at which things moved was quite exhilarating.

We were very fortunate at the beginning as the cricket season was looming and we had no home ground. We thought we would have to be one of those wandering sides, but that would have meant changing the club name. There was a lot of discussion about it as nobody really wanted a different name – if anything sets us cricketers apart it's our sense of tradition – and somehow 'The Ferret and Firkin Nomads CC' had a nasty taste about it (not to mention 'The Homeless Ferrets CC' and 'The Firkin Wanderers CC').

But Mr Gloomburg saved the day by persuading another pub side to let us have their ground – if you can call a northern extension of Hampstead Heath a ground. It was rumoured that he had the wherewithal on the club chairman and secretary over some shady business dealings (apparently they were into ladies' underwear) but we never asked. We were so grateful for the ground.

The next step was to arrange fixtures and this was solved mainly by pinching those of the other club. I say 'mainly' because some of them looked decidedly iffy. To be quite honest none of us fancied playing The Mantovani Appreciation Society CC, The Gay Whales Against The Bomb CC, The Old Danny La Rueians CC, or The George Davis Is Innocent OKCC. But then this is South Hampstead and maybe we should have been more broadminded.

In the midst of all this we had our first general meeting. It was a grand occasion, celebrated with vast quantities of Mr Gloomburg's latest invention – a mixture of Southern Comfort and grapefruit juice with a splash of surgical spirit – and the pub favoured us with another extension.

Oh, what high hopes we had at that first meeting!

We even organised a constitution, rules of the club, patrons of the club, a management committee and match fees, well before last orders was rung.

On the list of patrons you'll be glad to know that you were top of the list. We would have let you know earlier, but nobody was quite sure which hospital you were in. Should you accept this position, any contribution would be gratefully accepted. In your case I think a First Aid kit would be appropriate.

The only thing remaining now was to buy the club kit. Our fund-raising only allowed us to buy the bare necessities.

Frankly we were amazed at the prices. Long gone are the days when you could buy a reasonable bat with a crate of empty Tizer bottles; and for the price they're asking for Graham Gooch batting gloves you'd think the great man was still wearing them. But here again we were lucky, Lucky.

On our management committee we have Big Al, the pub Casanova – remember him? He now lives with three lovely young ladies who are known as 'Al's Angels'. Well, Big Al knew a lady whose husband was into Army Surplus sportswear, so he reckoned he could get us all we needed, and very cheaply too, so we left the matter with him.

What we ended up with certainly did the job, but we had a hell of a time getting the camouflage off the stumps and the webbing off the pads. The umpires' coats were whitewashed flak-jackets with six bullets each in a shoulder pocket, but with all those extra pockets and belts and things they're perfect for the job. The bag which holds everything, for the moment, is an old rocket launcher case.

And so we were ready for our first game – against a North London Deaf Team – but I'll fill you in on that later.

The 1985 season has now finished and winter is drawing in. The only way I can tell that is because the rain is getting colder.

Hope you're feeling better, Lucky. Always remember John Boot who, at Newark in 1737, died after a collision with his batting partner.

Best wishes and good health,

Steve.

P.S. Preparation H is still your best bet.

3· *The Jewel in the Crown Tandoori (Coalite) Menu*

14 December 1985

Dear Lucky,

My dear old friend, how my heart bleeds for you! To have suffered as you have for all this time and now to be faced with this present indignity . . . I'm tempted to say that it serves you right but I feel so sorry for you.

I made the long journey yesterday to your present hospital, with a carrier bag full of old *Wisdens*, only to be turned away by a harridan of a ward sister saying that you had been put into isolation – in a children's ward at that. When she told me what had happened I must admit that I was filled with admiration.

It is typical of your good and caring nature to want to make life easier for those poor unfortunate children in hospital; and organising an In-Ward Children's Cricket Tournament was an admirable idea – but didn't you know that you'd never had mumps?

And how will this affect the treatment of the goitre?

You remind me of one of my great cricketing heroes: Lionel, Lord Tennyson, who led England at Leeds in 1921 and scored 63 with one arm in a sling. I'll try to get his book for you. It's called *From Verse to Worse*.

But not to worry, mate. I understand that the BBC will be doing their Christmas morning *Play School* programme from your hospital ward. When Santa comes to you, you might ask him for *The Boy's Own Annual of Cricketing Heroes* – it's usually pretty good value. And I have it from a very good source that because of various cutbacks at the Beeb there's a good chance that Santa will be played by Peter West this year. So put on a good face, because all at the Ferret and Firkin will be glued to the screen when they show the highlights.

Anyway, as I told you before, the Ferret and Firkin CC was eventually established and a brand new cricket team was about to wreak havoc on the English summer scene.

What hopes we had in those wintry-spring days! Cricket is such stuff as dreams are made on and our dreams were great indeed.

No goal was too high and even before our first game we dreamt of reaching the National Pub Cricket Team Final at Lord's; that is, until someone pointed out that there is no such thing – and anyway it would have been wasted on us as most of the wickets we were to play on were slightly worse than the queuing area at the Lord's Tavern Stand Bar.

Cricket is a social occasion and it seems to me to be the most perfect of places to discuss the world and its problems – in fact, the only civilised way in the most civilised of settings. This is reflected in all levels of society – as I witnessed when I was fortunate enough to get a glimpse of that Nirvanah, that ultimate dream of all pub cricketers – the Members' Bar at Lord's.

Admittedly it was only the briefest of glimpses, as I was so overcome with emotion and envy (and had to get out quickly before anyone caught me) but it did my heart proud to have got so close to this dream of dreams.

There were the Members, the nobility of cricket, all wearing those famous ties. If the Victoria Cross was made from Sevastopol's captured cannons then those ties must have been cut from some similar trophy. I like to think that the Lord's ground was fought for and won from a troupe of Maypole dancers. And the fact that most of the Members, while the cricket raged outside, were either doing the *Standard* kiddies' crossword or watching the Wimbledon tennis on television, whilst imbibing, only lends weight to my arguments about the sociability of cricket.

Anyway, so it was with high hopes that we adjourned from the Tap Room of the Ferret and Firkin on the eve of our first match, to the Jewel in the Crown Tandoori (Coalite) Restaurant around the corner for our first selection meeting.

There was no shortage of volunteers willing to take part in this first, and perhaps historic game.

Fingers Ashton immediately commandeered the piano and began to play selections from the menu. He started with 'When the Red, Red Raita Comes Pop-Popadoming Along' and went on to a main course of (à la Frank Ifield), 'I'll Re-Vindaloo-oo' with a side dish of Beethoven's 'Moonlight' Pyratha.

On the back of another menu the first ever team sheet was drawn up.

This is now the club's most treasured possession and stands framed in an honoured position on the Tap Room wall, spotlighted between the dartboard and the Gents'. To this lowly pub cricket team it is as revered as the Ashes themselves and exactly the same colour (a shade of Ceylon Meat Madras, the result of an unfortunate accident during an argument over the bill).

At the top of the team sheet, standing proudly, is the club's motto. We borrowed this from the Olympic Games (we didn't think they'd mind) as it seemed to sum up the aspirations held by all of us on that evening: '*Citius, altius, fortius*' ('Faster, higher, stronger').

Unfortunately, in retrospect, it seems to sum up more accurately the team's drinking attributes rather than any sporting ones – the faster we drink the higher we get and the stronger we think we are.

Here is the line-up for the first ever Ferret and Firkin CC game with a few comments about the players. I know that you know some of them and you'll probably recognise the rest:

1. **Gloomburg W. G.** (Capt.)
   The team's founder and mentor. A great organisational mind wrought from years in the advertising business. He was unanimously elected our first captain because of his ability to fool most of the people most of the time. At

present he is trying to convince a company called Seamans that it would be unwise to build a factory in Staines.
Ambition: to become Minister of Propaganda.

2. Sean Kildare, Dr

An Irish gynaecologist and steady opening bat. Master of the delicate hook and a keen eye for every delivery. A great judge and partaker of Mr Gloomburg's invented drinks, especially if containing Jameson's Whiskey, and a severe critic of what he calls, 'Cooking Lager' (Australian). Beneath all this, though, there lies a great romantic.
Ambition: to die in a duel after being caught in 'my lady's chamber'.

3. Dr Richard Payne, GP ('The General')

After studying the medical reports from all Napoleon's battles, he decided that he owed his livelihood to the great little man and subsequently adopted many of his characteristics. Is forever discussing tactics, drawing up plans of attack and offering advice to anyone who is daft enough to listen, including the opposition. Had to be persuaded that to field at first slip with one arm inside your jumper is just not on, though he adopted this stance with great success as an umpire.
Ambition: to get to Waterloo as soon as possible after the pub shuts.

4. Big Al

The pub Casanova and All Right Guy. A very high scorer, due to his innate ability to pull anything. At one game played at Finsbury Park, he was fielding at deep fine leg for us and at third slip with his back to the bowler in the game on the next pitch. Even so, he still managed to arrange a date with second slip's sister who was watching the game.
Ambition: to score 1,000 in a season.

5. Morley, S. J. (myself)

From a long line of Yorkshire cricket fanatics. My father and his father before him used to sell cushions at Headingley. When Dad was eight years old he was standing by the

DAVE THE GRAVE

steps which led to the Players' Dining Room and Wally Hammond stepped out. On seeing the little waif, W. H. said, 'Come here, son.' Dad approached, mouth open and eyes wide with hero worship. 'You see that meal there,' said Wally, as Dad now calls him, 'you take it away and eat it. I'm not hungry.' Dad was overawed. To be given the food off his hero's plate – and the plate as well! He showed it to Granddad who said, 'Ta lad,' and promptly ate the lot.
Ambition: to become an MCC member and get to the bar as quickly as possible (though not necessarily in that order).

6. **Cronin, A.** (known as 'Cronin the Librarian')
His great strength and fearful Neolithic grin have put fear into many a close fielder and turned him into a tactical batsman – he swings like hell at anything and sometimes gets lucky. He is a great favourite of our two doctors who have persuaded him to leave his body to science.
Ambition: not to be out first ball.

7. **Dick Dickinson**
The straight-haired, Brylcreemed West Indian all-rounder: 48 years old, 48-inch waist and 48 inches tall. A garage mechanic often confused for the team mascot and in his whites confused for a *Minstrel Show* Michelin Man. The team's all-rounder because he's totally useless at everything. He reckons he knows everything but in fact he knows absolutely nothing, as witnessed when he refers to 'sight-screams' and 'medium-space bowling'.
Ambition: to make everybody stop patting him on the head.

8. **Dave the Grave**
6ft 11 in tall, wedding photographer's nightmare and expert curtain fitter. A slow thinker with extremely slow reactions. Often brought on to bowl in order to terrorise good batsmen, but frequently forgets to let go of the ball. Dave has brought a new word into the English language: 'Nyer'. This precedes everything he says and can mean 'yes' or 'no'

or 'don't know'. He looks at life from deep third man rather than from slips. Absolutely no ambitions whatsoever.

9. Romeley S. Vet

An actor who sounds like the only anagram in the team. He changed his name for professional purposes after making a brief appearance as the vet in *Emmerdale Farm*. In this job his right arm found itself in many sticky places which has helped to make him a useful quick bowler, if only he can get the line right. His introduction to cricket came whilst filming *Emmerdale* when he was asked to play in a charity match at Windhill CC, Shipley. He approached this first game as he would a great Shakespearean role and after eight overs he broke his collar bone whilst attempting a suicidal catch at long on. The next scene he filmed was a snogging scene with Sandy outside the cowshed in a car. The tears in his eyes as he slipped his arm around her led one lady in a Bradford curry house to describe it as the most romantic performance since Valentino. He is an enthusiastic fielder, flinging himself dramatically at anything which leads to a general cry of 'RADA!' from his team-mates.

Ambition: to be asked to play for The Lord's Taverners.

10. Typhoon Turnbull

Let's not be coy about this: this man is a psychopath. an Australian fast bowler who models himself not so much on Lillee as on Rambo. He takes great pride in being as revolting as possible, his favourite food being raw garlic and baked beans. He is a leading member of a local chapter of the Hell's Angels known as 'The Beelzebub Bashers of Botham'. Looking at him you realise why there is an Australian lager called 'XXXX': because Australians can't spell 'Beer'.

Ambition: to get away with six beamers every over.

11. Fingers Ashton

Wicket-keeper and pub pianist, often confusing the two. An accomplished songwriter singer with a unique one-handed style when it comes to the 'fiddly bits' – thus leaving a hand free for his pint. A great Tap Room character who had a No. 2 hit record in 1971 and has been celebrating ever since.

Ambition: to break off diplomatic relations with the Official Receiver and to make a stumping.

Scorer: **the lovely Jan**

Jan is beautiful. Her scorebook is a joy to look at. From a family of seven brothers and a cricket-mad father. Wendy Wimbush eat your heart out.

Ambition: to be a first-class umpire.

Our combined ages come to 466 which is, by coincidence, the same number of pints downed by us in an average week.

Funnily enough, there wasn't a Londoner in the team – which is about par for South Hampstead.

By the Lord Benaud we were proud that night, the eve of our first game.

The Tap Room was alive with anticipation.

The local launderette was awash with whites.

For now, Lucky, take care, and don't eat all your selection boxes at once. Have a Happy Christmas. Cheers from the Tap Room at the Ferret and Firkin where we will drink to your health,

Steve.

4· *The First Game*

4 January 1986

Dear Lucky,

By the lords of Harley Street it was good to hear that you're back on the mend. I don't know what they put in your Christmas Complan but it must have done you the world of good.

When we saw the highlights of the Christmas Day *Play School* programme you looked positively glowing with health, you little tinker you. You were actually smiling when Santa gave you your present.

But what was it? They missed any shots of you opening it. Not that you could in an oxygen tent.

At the moment there is great debate in the Tap Room. Dick Dickinson is taking bets and there is some quite heavy money being placed. The consensus is that the present is a very small book of some kind and these are the odds you can get:

1–3: *Dicky Bird's Book of Peacock Recipes*
4–5: *The 1986 Australian Good Lager Guide*
Evens: *The Fred Trueman Book of Etiquette*
5–4 *A Smile For Every Occasion* by Craig MacDermott
2–1: *Ian Botham's Book of Pot Plants*
7–2 *The Denis Lillee and Rodney Marsh Book of Test Match Betting Tents* (Headingley Press)
3–1: *The Greg Chappell Guide To Underarm Bowling*
5–1: *How To Win Friends And Influence People* by G. Boycott Esq.
10–1: *South African Memoirs* by Basil D'Oliveira
33–1: *The Colin Milburn Weightwatchers' Guide*

Please let us know what it was, and could you also let us know who Santa was? I was told it would be Peter West and it could well have been. After every 'Ho, ho, ho,' he did look round for a monitor to see what the hell was happening and there was that same bemused expression, especially when that little girl piddled on his foot.

Big Al reckoned it was Wendy Wimbush but I think that was just wishful thinking.

Anyway, a wonderful Christmas was had by all in the Tap Room.

Big Al was the only real injury, after an unfortunate incident with a nutcracker which put him out of action for some time.

The main joy was the Christmas tasting of Mr Gloomburg's concoctions. By the lords of Watneys we had a rare old time with those. As the night grew long I believe that a mixture of Creme de Menthe, tomato juice and malt whisky proved a popular winner, though I really don't remember much about it. Whatever it was, it was christened 'The Scottish Pope's Revenge'.

I think that on this particular Christmas many of us could have died happy (I'm not so sure some of us didn't), totally at one with life, sitting there in our beloved Tap Room, surrounded by great friends, the walls festooned with decorations adorning the Cricket Club Mementos – the first team sheet, Julie the Club Jug etc.

We had a wonderful imitation-log gas fire roaring in the hearth and we were full of the spirits of Christmas. In years to come archeologists may discover us and take this to be the perfect example of life as lived by South Hampstead Man – *Homo Blottus Ferret Ferkinus.*

One was reminded of much earlier days when Anglo-Saxons would sit in their long cabins (or long rooms), feasting and telling tales of old. On one such occasion a sparrow came in at one end of the hall, flew the length of the room and disappeared through the hole in the wall at the other end. All witnessed this. Nobody knew from whence it had come and nobody knew where it was going. The local sage stood up and likened this to the meaning of life: we don't know where we're from or where we're going. The rest of them, as it happens, thought it was sod all to do with them, threw the silly bugger out into the cold and had a game of indoor cricket.

Such was the mood one day when we remembered the first game played by the newly formed Ferret and Firkin CC. By this time, of course, the game had become part of the Tap Room folklore and the stories were becoming exaggerated, to say the least.

But I can remember the day of that game vividly.

The night before had been spent in the Jewel in the Crown Tandoori (Coalite) Restaurant around the corner. Along with the vast amount of curried delicacies consumed that night, many pints of Indian beer were also put away. This particularly evil brew was concocted by some retired hippies in Jodhpur. When you opened the mud-encrusted bottle it made a sound rather like a recently chimed mantra and tasted like Ghandi's flip-flop. The colour was the same as the Ganges on washing day and I'm sure Gungadin must have been drinking it when he got killed.

Anyway, the next morning we looked like the survivors from Napoleon's Moscow outing. I know that I had a mouth like a gorilla's armpit.

The only one who felt great was the Ozzie psychopath Typhoon Turnbull, who said it reminded him of when he used to eat live dingos. He then had several pints of Ozzie lager *nouveau* to wash it down and made me realise that the only difference between Australians and yoghurt is that only one of them has a live culture.

As we prepared to leave for the match I couldn't help thinking that it was a good thing we had two doctors on the side – though what the gynaecologist could do was anybody's guess.

Dr Payne said that Napoleon was often ill before a battle and then, as if to prove it, disappeared into the Gents'.

Mr Gloomburg was busily concocting new drinks guaranteed to get rid of a hangover – probably because they got you so drunk you forgot all about it.

Big Al began a long round of goodbyes to most of the ladies

in the pub and when Dave the Grave was stopped from using Dick Dickinson as a basketball we were ready for battle.

Indeed, when the Army Surplus cricket gear emerged you would have thought we were more like weekend soldiers than weekend cricketers.

The biggest problem was to get people to leave. After years of serious service to the Tap Room a kind of inborn clock had come to regulate our behaviour. With still an hour to go before last orders many a right arm was motioning towards the mouth instead of motioning towards the door.

Many of us have asked the same question: what on earth were we doing? Eleven assorted hangovers playing cricket?

It looked like it would snow too.

The team we were to play was a Deaf Team from North London. The General said that reconnaissance reports suggested that their opening bat was one Mr Kapil Deaf.

Dick Dickinson wondered what the tea would be like and Big Al wondered the same about the tea-ladies.

When we arrived at their council-owned ground there was a groan of disappointment as we realised that there was no clubhouse – which meant that there was no bar.

That proved to be the least of our worries.

After we had emerged from what was laughingly called a dressing room (I believe it had been used for coal hoarding during the General Strike) some of us went to inspect the pitch.

Now it is fair to say that none of us had played cricket for donkey's years and our love and experience of the game was derived mainly from *Test Match Special* and BBC 2 highlights. The lack of 20,000 people to cheer us on we could cope with but the absence of a scoreboard, sight-screens and the New Tavern Stand Bar sent some of us into a mild state of shock which possibly accounted for the ensuing dismal performance.

Most shocking of all was the pitch.

As this was the first game of the season it followed that it overlapped with the final games of the football season. This had obviously caused the groundsman with a shortage of space some worries. The strip had quite ingeniously been placed alongside the goal-line of the football pitch next door. Obviously a game had been played there that morning as that 'little patch of rough outside the off-stump' looked like a First World War trench system. Fortunately the goal posts had been removed, as indicated by two holes in the ground. Furthermore, if you were unfortunate enough to be fielding at deep third man you were in danger of being maimed in a Rugby scrum.

We lost the toss and were put into bat.

The opposition were a great set of lads and obviously knew how to take advantage of the intricacies of their pitch. We were all out for 28, the highest score being someone called Extras with 24.

There were more ducks than you'll find in the lobby of a Peking café.

When the last man, Fingers Ashton, was clean-bowled walking away from a ball that pitched six feet outside his off-stump, we hung our heads.

As everybody walked off, Dick Dickinson was gesticulating wildly to Fingers to show him how he should have played the shot. Unfortunately, in deaf sign language this meant that all the fielders were lesbians who were suffering from various anti-social diseases and a fight nearly broke out.

Tea was postponed as it hadn't even been bought yet, let alone prepared.

It also began to snow.

We took to the field freezing cold and miserable.

The General tried to raise morale but it was hopeless.

As the openers went into double figures, Fingers Ashton, keeping wicket, decided on 'tactics'. The large amount of Spinach Vindaloo consumed the night before was having a dramatic effect on his innards and as he crouched close behind the wicket a series of loud reports erupted from beneath his pads. This, I must admit, seemed to be our only chance of winning until Fingers was seriously reprimanded by Mr Gloomburg for ungentlemanly conduct. Fingers complained bitterly that it didn't matter anyway because the batsman couldn't hear them. True, agreed Mr Gloomburg, but he could sure as hell smell them.

After three overs the game was over.

The possibility of a second innings was discussed and then rejected because the snow was falling heavily and would eventually present an unfair advantage to the fielders who would be camouflaged by it.

Our first game had lasted less than an hour.

Only two people had made any runs.

Nobody had taken a wicket or a catch.

A blizzard raged.

And it was four hours before the pub opened.

This definitely was not cricket.

For now, Lucky, take care,

Steve.

5· 'Pub Cricket'

29 January 1986

Dear Lucky,

I just couldn't believe it when they told me – German measles?

Didn't you have all these diseases when you were young? You'll be coming down with diphtheria next, or nappy rash. At least you can't have any teething problems, as you had all them pulled out years ago.

Do sort yourself out, mate. The new season is really not that far away and we'd like to see you back in time. I have to prepare you for a few shocks though.

I know Lucky, that when it comes to this noble game of ours you are a true gent and within the Ferret and Firkin CC we have tried to maintain the same ideals. This has been a very difficult task indeed as we have come into contact with a level of cricket which I know you find unacceptable. I believe it was a reason for your retirement but it is much worse than it was then.

In my ignorance I always thought that cricket divided itself into four basic levels: international, county, club and village. There were always others which were beneath contempt: I speak mainly of circus cricket and French cricket (trust the frogs to misunderstand the LBW rules). But there is a fifth level which plays a very important part in the English summer scene, and we were far from prepared for it.

After our first disastrous game we returned to the Tap Room, eventually, in a state of shock. The General tried to raise morale but all his tactics talk made us even more depressed.

Fortunately Cronin the Librarian side-tracked him into a

discussion by asking him to use his medical knowledge to define the difference between fear and sex. The General embarked on a lengthy monologue quoting Napoleon, Freud and Jean Harlow. He then asked Cronin why he wished to know.

'Well,' said Cronin, to the delight of all who listened, 'I always thought that the difference between fier and sex was funf.'

But if we were depressed that night you should have seen us after our first encounter with this fifth level of cricket.

I am talking of course, about 'pub cricket'. I know we're based in a pub but this really took us aback. So shocked were we that Romeley S. Vet, the actor, burst into tears. I tried to console him but it was hopeless. All he could say was, 'Hercules cried, Ajax cried, Lear and Cyrano cried. My dear chap, it's in the best heroic tradition.'

Now pub cricket is a game all to itself. Whilst ignoring all the traditions of the game it maintains all the traditions of the pub. At best it acquires a kind of soporific blend.

I believe that it all came about with the inception of Sunday licensing hours and cheap air flights from Australia. It is about how to while away those hours in a civilised fashion while still pretending you're in the pub.

This is not the traditional game of batsman pitted against bowler.

It revolves around what I believe to be an Australian innovation (it had to be): a large plastic box with a handle known as a 'cooler'. A minimum of two coolers are placed in strategic positions around the ground, usually on top of each other behind the wickets, and then both fielders and batsmen alike are placed in such a way as to prevent the ball from hitting them. You will gauge the measure of my contempt when I say that each cooler contains vast amounts of cans of (usually Australian) lager. These, within the mythology of pub cricket, have become known as 'tubes'.

Around all this some semblance of a game of cricket takes place.

Alas, the biggest shock of all is to find that all the traditional terms of the game have a totally new meaning. We played, unfortunately, rather a lot of pub cricket last season and I managed to make a list. Incomplete as it is, it may give you an idea of what I am talking about.

But then again it may not.

Wicket-keeper: Protector of the cooler
Batsman: First line of cooler protection
Bowler: Main threat to the cooler
Slow bowler: A drunken bowler
Fast bowler: Lunatic from the Temperance League
Box: The cooler ('Are you wearing a box?' means 'Have you enough tubes for the game?')
Mid wicket: The middle wicket behind which opened tubes are placed.
Popping crease: Where champagne bottles are opened.
Boundary: The Gents'
Clubhouse: The pub
Strip: Occurring in the pub before match
Novice: When there is no strip
Little patch of rough: The club secretary's mistress
Sight-screens: See 'Boundary'
Game: See 'Little patch of rough'
Ball: Cricket club dinner
No ball: Cricket club dinner cancelled
Wide ball, beamer and high ball: Cocktails
W. G. Grace: Another cocktail (wine, gin and a prayer)
Pitch: Guinness
Bails: Irish Cream
Swing: Sweet Wine in Glass
Bye: 'It's your round!'
Leg bye: 'Walk to the bar and get them in!'
Tea-ladies: Bar maids
Long hop: An away game
On drive: The away game is on
Off drive: The away game is cancelled
Inside and outside edge: When the ball just missed the cooler

Leg glance: Ogling the tea-ladies
A slight tickle: Occurs after a 'Leg Glance'
Pull: Opening a tube (nothing to do with 'A slight tickle')
Gulley: See 'Boundary'
A slash outside the off stump: See 'Boundary'
Slips: When the contents of a tube are spilled
Mid-off: A stomach upset
Silly mid-off: A stomach upset from mixing your drinks
Fine leg: Last line of cooler defence
Third man: An after-hours Austrian drinking club
Night watchman: A timekeeper who warns when a pub is about to open
Covers: Whites
Short extra cover: A sleeveless sweater
Scorer: The pub Casanova
LBW: Lager Behind Wicket
Hit wicket: A drunken batsman
Run out: The cooler is empty
Runner: Someone who leaves the ground after a 'Run Out'
Out: You've had too much to drink
Not out: You're still standing
Obstruction: Barred from the 'Clubhouse'
Clean-bowled: Tubes behind the wicket or the Cooler are hit
Stumps: Siting Tubes Under My Pads
Discussing the state of play: Counting the empty tubes
Hook: Golf practice
End of over: Time for a drink
Bad light stopped play: The 'Clubhouse' was open
Rain stopped play: Ditto
Limited overs: The game ended before the 'Clubhouse' was open
Teamsheet: List of who owns what in the cooler
Roller: The pub gambler
Heavy roller: Addicted 'Roller'
Umpire: The landlord
Win: A tea-lady
Playing for a win: See 'Leg Glance'

Changing room: See 'Boundary'
Draw: The club raffle
Tie: Totally Inebriated Experience
Start of play: When the pub closes
Close of play: When the pub opens
Match abandoned: Too drunk to play
Playing for a draw: Making the drink last
Follow through: Downing a pint in one
Follow on: Downing a yard of ale in one
Four: A four-pack
Six: A six-pack
Runs: See 'Silly Mid-Off'
5 Wickets or 50 runs = 1 Jug
10 Wickets or 100 runs = 2 jugs, etc.
Bat: The club secretary's wife
Kit bag: The club secretary's wife's cat
Boots: The First-Aid kit (usually just a bottle of brandy)
Pads: Protected Areas of Drinker's Skin
Pads up: Ditto Unless Piddled
Thigh pad: A hip-flask
Protective helmet: A prophylactic

UMPIRE'S SIGNALS
'Out' = 'Yes thank you, just one Tube please.'
'No ball' = 'Get my friend a drink.'
'Wide' = 'Get both my friends a drink.'
'Short run' = 'A glass with a handle please.'
'Four' = 'Forget the last order.'
'Six' = 'The drinks are on me.'
'Bye' = 'Any chance of getting a drink?'
'Dead ball' = 'Forget the G and T – the wife's changed her
  mind again.'
'Leg bye' = 'Let's have a knees-up.'

And so on.
Unfortunately there are more.
The first pub cricket game we played was against a team

called The Crown and Sceptre. To remember this, Mr Gloomburg invented a new drink ('Lest we forget,' he said). It
consisted of one part of each of every Australian lager we
could find with two parts Meths added to give it some taste; it
is known in the Tap Room as a 'Colon and Sphincter Cocktail'.
Like the game we had just played, it was absolutely vile.
For now old friend, take care and good health,

Steve.

6· *'Lord's Prayer'*

13 February 1986

Dear Lucky,

I was so pleased to hear that you had eventually left the children's ward. Having all those kid's diseases must have been traumatic for you, but at least you've got them out of the way now, so you shouldn't be troubled again.

That they should have such an effect on your eyes is, I am assured, only psychosomatic, but it should teach those kids to behave themselves and have a little respect for their elders.

I am told that your pleas and ministrations were heartrending when the whole ward decided to use your bed as a trampoline; and really, that was no way in which to treat an NHS potty.

And don't you worry about not being able to read those old *Wisdens* I had sent round, for you must always remember the diagnosis of the great Dr Grace himself: 'Reading ruins batting.'

Did you know that there are cricket teams established now for blind people? I must admit that I found it difficult to swallow at first, but believe me it's true and all rather wonderful. Of course it's not the usual game and has been modified accordingly. All they do is take a large soft ball which has an electronic bleeper inside it, so that the players can hear where it is, and everything else is more or less normal. The wonders of modern science, eh?

I was telling this to the crowd in the Tap Room the other day and some of them didn't believe me. But the General assured them that it was perfectly true. He went on to tell the story of a junior doctor of his acquaintance who was working for a school for the blind in Yorkshire.

This man was asked to supervise a trip to the seaside with about twenty-five of the patients. He gratefully accepted, as he needed a day out himself, but on arriving he was at a loss as to what to do with them all.

He managed to get them all on to the beach when he remembered an article he had read about 'Blind Cricket'. Knowing that all these people were cricket-mad anyway he decided that this would be a great idea.

Unfortunately he didn't possess the technical equipment, so he had to improvise. He bought a plastic football and a pair of ladies' tights. He then borrowed half a dozen small bells from the man who ran the donkey rides, who was more than pleased to help. By placing the bells in the tights and then wrapping them around the football, he had created the 'cricket ball'.

Everyone on the beach was intrigued and there were many helpers. By searching the beach for driftwood they found many adequately sized pieces to use as bats and wickets.

The teams were organised and battle commenced. It was a huge success and a small crowd assembled to cheer the participants along.

Seeing that all was proceeding perfectly well, the young doctor decided that it was safe to sneak off for a quick pint. He had not been away for more than ten minutes when a man came running into the pub in a state of great panic looking for him.

'What on earth's the matter?' asked the doctor, fearing the worst.

'Come quickly,' said the man, 'it's your batsmen – they're battering the local Morris dancers to death!'

Now as our first season progressed we found ourselves playing, much to our distress, quite a lot of 'pub cricket'.

To most of us this was an abomination and the temptation of diving into the opposition's coolers, when requested, was often too much for some. The worst offender was the Aussie, Typhoon Turnbull, whose eyes glazed over at the sight of so much Australian cooking lager.

The more of these 'teams' we played the worse things became and it took a stroke of genius from our mentor, Mr Gloomburg, to stop the rot.

With all his magnetic powers of leadership he convinced us that it was our bold and honoured duty to uphold the principles of our noble game. From then on we approached each game of pub cricket as if it were a crusade. We became like missionaries of old embarking on a quest to teach righteousness to the heathen.

As we were situated in South Hampstead, a mere mile and a half away from the sacred ground of Lord's itself, our task of saving the game became all the more important.

When we took to the field against a pub team we became avenging angels, nay, disciples spreading the word.

Before each game Mr Gloomburg would gather us round. We would doff our caps, gaze respectfully in the general direction of Lord's and he would lead us in what has become known as 'Lord's Prayer':

> *Pub Cricket,*
> *A drunk eleven,*
> *Boozing be thy game.*
> *Thy fielding's dumb,*
> *To drink you come*
> *On fields that should be held sacred.*
> *Give us, Oh Lord's, a decent game*
> *And save us all hesitation,*
> *And we will show them*
> *How the game should be played.*
> *Lead us not unto the cooler*
> *And deliver us to victory.*
> *For thine is the birth right,*
> *The Long Room not the Tap Room,*
> *For over and over,*
> *Amen.*

We would then proceed to knock hell out of them, stipulating every rule of the game and enthusing about the glory of cricket.

The wonder of all was Typhoon Turnbull. Mr Gloomburg channelled and trained all that psychopathic energy into a mean machine. He filled him with heroic tales; of how Harold Larwood would partake of a pint of ale *before* a game to give him strength and of how Fred Trueman made beer commercials. This instilled in Typhoon the urge to emulate these heroes and effectively stopped him from drinking during a game. (He insisted on having a drink before the game though – the nearest equivalent to Larwood's pint being three Aussie ones.) He developed into a bowler of alarming proportions – Rambo in whites – and woe betide any batsman who placed a can of booze behind his stumps. Typhoon's Yorker became known as 'the Typhoon Tuber'.

The rest of the team developed similar attributes.

Sean Kildare could produce a hook which would guide the ball behind him at an alarming rate and smash any coolers that stood in the way.

Big Al perfected the straight upward drive so that it would also devastate the opposite cooler. In one innings they amassed a quick 50-run partnership made up entirely from 5 runs from each scoring hit.

Romeley S. Vet, the actor, on taking any quick single, would overshoot the opposite crease, falling dramatically, like a felled Richard III, into any stray cans that lay about.

Watching all these cans of Aussie lager *nouveau* being split and spilt around the field did my heart proud and I must admit that I myself developed some quite handy tricks. It's amazing how these cans squash so easily. It was almost worth hitting your own wicket to see the cans assembled behind go splattering to the ground spilling their contents everywhere. If you were out you could always come back on and umpire, and the chances of mischief then were manifold especially if, like the General, you could quote alcoholism figures at the fielders.

Of course, all this was done in the most gentlemanly manner.

If a can, or better still, a cooler was quite accidentally smashed to smithereens we became most apologetic and the team was always invited back to the Ferret and Firkin Tap Room for riotous drinking in its proper setting.

W. G. GLOOMBURG
— (CAPT.) —

Most of the time they needed a drink anyway.

After our first such outing Romeley misquoted Eliot perfectly: 'We were the Hollow Men, Now they are the Stuffed Men.'

In all of this Mr Gloomburg reigned supreme and, along with the General, his second-in-command whether he needed him or not, we wreaked havoc on these wayward pub sides. He even took out shares in a local cooler-making company, astutely realising that if this destruction continued he could make a fortune.

Also, I will never forget their patience with Cronin the Librarian. For several evenings after work they conducted secret training sessions with him, developing what they called 'a strike of unsurpassed beauty'.

When it came to our next game, Cronin opened the batting.

The first ball was delivered harmlessly outside off-stump and he swung wildly towards leg. At the height of his amazing follow-through he let go of the bat, which sailed some forty-five feet into the air and came crashing down with alarming violence on top of the cooler placed behind the keeper.

The cooler splattered into a hundred pieces. Cans exploded, frothing wildly. And, to top it all, the ball sailed away for four of the most dramatic runs scored at any level of cricket.

A collage of these cooler pieces was assembled in the shape of four Xs and now stands framed among our other treasures on the Tap Room wall. It is dated and titled: 'The Cronin Cooler Crusher'.

Well, Lucky, I wish you could have been there to see all this, but never mind, we're hoping to see you soon – and hoping too of course, that you can see us.

We had a collection for you and we've bought you this lucky rabbit's foot which you'll find enclosed. You could do with some good fortune.

For now, be good,

Steve.

P.S. I've just realised that you won't be able to read this. Oh well, never mind, I'm sure you'll sort something out. Take care.

7· *The Australians Come to South Hampstead*

23 February 1986

Dear Lucky,

My dear friend, I cannot tell you how sorry I am. My heart bleeds for you, it really does.

The mood in the Tap Room is one of deep regret and sorrow. We feel as though we have just been trounced by a team playing on pogo sticks.

But honestly Lucky, we never meant any harm.

It was with great admiration and affection that we had the whip-round and bought the lucky rabbit's foot for you. We even had it engraved: 'To Lucky. From all at the Tap Room.' Everyone thought it was a lovely gesture and believe me Lucky, none of us had any idea that myxomatosis still existed. Honest.

But I am told that modern science can deal with it quite adequately now, so you should be all right. We hope so anyway.

As the new season looms closer we are looking forward with great anticipation to carrying on with our crusade against what we nicknamed 'pub cricket'.

Now don't get me wrong, Lucky; we are not purists and we don't take the game so seriously that it becomes unenjoyable. We just believe that even at our level of cricket certain standards have to be upheld. We are not playing in a games room, nor are we playing in the Bradford League. We just believe that 'pub cricket' is to the game what Lester Piggott is to piles.

There is, on the other hand, the type of team that takes the game so seriously that it spoils all the fun. At our level a delicate balance has to be struck. We're not in a league, for heaven's sake: all our games are supposed to be friendlies. We did, however, play several of these teams last season.

The worst one was against a North London Synagogue Eleven. The game had been arranged by Mr Gloomburg himself, and it had promised to be a lovely occasion.

Unfortunately their behaviour was appalling. There was fighting and arguments and foul language – the sort of behaviour you wouldn't expect to find outside New South Wales. All of this went on within their own team – they hardly acknowledged us at all. That is, apart from one occasion when the General, who was umpiring, turned down three successive appeals from a particularly aggressive bowler. He motioned up to the General and said, 'What would you do if I call you a bastard?'

'Young man,' said the General, 'I would immediately report you to your captain for ungentlemanly conduct.'

'I am the captain,' said the bowler.

'In that case I would refer the matter to our captain and we would discuss it further.'

The bowler then delivered a full toss which was dispatched with ease for four. He turned to the General and said, 'What if I thought you were a bastard?'

'Young man,' said the General, reasonably, 'what you think is of no concern to me in my capacity as umpire.'

'All right,' said the bowler, 'I think you're a bastard.'

Fortunately such teams are few and far between. I hope.

During the long Tap Room nights, in the light of the imitation-log gas fire, there were many discussions on the merits of playing such teams. I think that our standards had become so high that we were in danger of crossing off every one of the games on the fixture list – a 1930s MCC XI being the only team good enough.

In short, we were becoming cricketing snobs.

The one who put it all into perspective was Dave the Grave. Now Dave has never been known as a great contributor to our discussions, mainly because by the time he thinks of a point the subject has usually been changed. This time, however, he surprised us.

He began in his usual way.

'Nyer,' he said, which could have meant that he was enjoying his drink or was about to sneeze, 'I was once a teacher.'

The Tap Room fell into an astonished silence and we all looked up at him – even though he was sitting down we still had to look up at him.

'Nyer . . . I was a teacher at a progressive school and they refused to let the cricket team play in whites because they had abolished all aspects of uniform.'

More silence. More astonishment.

'Nyer . . . you see, each team sets its own limitations. Nyer . . . but it never stopped the kids enjoying themselves. After all, when all's said and done, it's only a game. Nyer . . .'

Well, after we'd all conjured with the idea of Dave as a teacher, we settled into taking his point; and it was made again the following day when we took up our customary positions in the New Tavern Stand at Lord's to witness Saturday's play in the Test Match.

If you remember, the day was quite thrilling for its cricket, but for us it was marred by long delays and stoppages – at the bar, that is. I don't know what it is about that bar, but over the years it has descended in quality so that it now possesses all the charm of an Australian sheep-shearing shed.

One old boy was so irate at having to queue forever for a pint of fizzy froth that he began to read *The Times'* obituary column out loud. When he did get to the bar he asked the barman which one of the names was his? The barman replied by asking him what he would do if drinking at cricket matches were banned (there was a lot of talk about this at the time).

'Cricket without drinking?' said the old boy. 'It could be the end of the game as we know it!'

However, after the close of play we returned to the Tap Room in great spirits where we discovered that a local pub was entertaining certain members of the Australian touring side.

This was an opportunity not to be missed.

We arrived at The Washington, a beautiful Victorian pub with a lovely atmosphere – not quite the Tap Room – but for South Hampstead with all its antiseptic pubs serving antiseptic beer to antiseptic people it wasn't bad.

Now the Australians on their tour here had been sponsored by a certain Aussie lager company: hence the proliferation of lurid yellow signs adorning our most beautiful cricket grounds throughout the summer. As part of their sponsorship contract the players were required to show themselves at certain times in pubs that sold the stuff. I must admit that in retrospect I would put this down as the main reason why they lost the Ashes.

When we entered, all the atmosphere of this lovely pub had disappeared.

What was occurring was nothing short of a circus. A huge crowd had assembled and the pub was bursting at the seams. There was a camera crew, photographers, models, a rock band, various hangers-on and three bemused looking cricketers, only one of whom had played that day. As the rock band set up their equipment the cricketers and models were jostled around them while the photographers tried to pose the mêlée.

Executives of the lager company tried to order everyone around for the sake of the camera crew. Then, as the band tested their equipment and the camera crew began to film, the executives thrust cans of lager into the hands of models and cricketers alike, whilst telling everybody to look as though they were enjoying themselves.

Unfortunately, all this overloaded the pub's electrical system and all the fuses blew.

Now this was superb, because it meant that the pumps that delivered this 'drink' couldn't work so the pub couldn't sell any of the stuff anyway. Eventually all was mended, but after five minutes of bright lights, forced smiles and general chaos the fuses blew again.

And again.

And again.

In the end, apparently satisfied, everyone disappeared to another pub, where presumably the same nonsense occurred again.

Now one of these cricketers was the young Australian great hope for the future, Craig MacDermott.

We had spent that day marvelling at this young man's obvious talents and commenting on his apparent lack of humour. I mean, the man never smiles, does he? The photographers managed it somehow, but then his mouth only quivered up and down for $^1/_{125}$th of a second at a time.

In the midst of all this, Romeley S. Vet, the actor, ever aware of a camera, managed to squirm his way up to the man and introduce himself.

'Hello,' he said, 'My name's Romeley and I bowl for a local team. I've been watching you play at Lord's today and I've got a few tips for you.'

The result of this attempted humour was a stare that I presume is usually reserved for David Gower. 'It was a joke,' pleaded Romeley, withering, only to be greeted with a stare reserved for Botham when he's just hit him for six.

'Bloody hell,' said Romeley afterwards, remembering Dave the Grave's commment, 'it's only a game.'

And that was how Dave's point was hammered home. To these chaps with those sort of pressures it's more than a game, but to us, it's there to be enjoyed and loved. (There is another moral of course: keep awful drink out of cricket.)

There was one other thing that happened.

As I wandered around this carnival I came to a little corner with a small table and a big man sitting at it. He was oblivious to all that was occurring around him as he read his book sitting quietly by himself. He would occasionally look up and laugh or sing a little tune to himself and then go back to his book.

It was the great Colin Milburn.

I took a deep breath and nervously introduced myself.

'Have you come to meet the players, Mr Milburn?' I asked, quite in awe at having met one of my cricketing heroes.

'Nay, bonny lad,' he replied, reaching for his pint of real ale, 'I've come to listen to the band.'

For now Lucky, good health.

Cheers!

Steve.

'Nay, bonny lad,' he replied, reaching for his pint of real ale, 'I've come to listen to the band.'

For now Lucky, good health.

8· Big Al and the Latter Day Saints CC

8 March 1986

Dear Lucky,

There was great celebration in the Tap Room last week when we heard that at long last you were coming out of hospital.

We were also overjoyed to hear that the myxomatosis was only psychosomatic.

It's been so long Lucky since that first day last year when you dropped into Casualty to have that boil lanced.

With the help of our two doctors, Mr Gloomburg invented a new Tap Room drink to celebrate your release. It was a mixture of two parts brandy for strength, one part orange juice for Vitamin C content, three parts poteen for the complexion and one part Benylin to help you breathe after you've swallowed it. It was called 'The Lucky Returns Cocktail'.

Everyone had little presents for you, not least of which was the extension arranged in your honour by the landlord (it's the fifteenth time this year that his daughter has got engaged).

Dick Dickinson invented a super little gadget in his garage which meant that by pulling certain strings you wouldn't have to leave your seat when it came to your round.

The two doctors arranged various screens and gadgets that were something to do with your colostomy and there were lots of other things ranging from a reinforced umpire's coat to the latest *Wisden* written in Braille. There was also a *Woman's Own* sewing kit in case your stitches came out again.

You can imagine our disappointment when we heard that for five hours you were stuck in the hospital lift with that stretcher case who was on his way down to Surgery. To have had to sit there for such a length of time in your condition was bad enough, but to have to watch that orderly perform an urgent appendectomy while the doctor shouted instructions from the floor below must have been horrendous for you. I'm not at all surprised that they took you back in for observation and treatment for shock – the only consolation being, I suppose, that your bed wasn't yet cold.

When the news came through it reminded us of one Sunday lunchtime just before a game when Big Al got stuck in something which nearly led to him missing the game.

Now, as the pub Casanova and All Right Guy, Al has certain responsibilities to uphold. One of these is to make sure that he never runs out of those little packets you buy from the bubble-gum machine in the Gents'.

Unfortunately, the week before, Al had broken a finger on his right hand attempting a most dramatic catch of Errol Flynn proportions in the covers. To keep his finger straight he had taped a plastic cradle to it and when he put his hand into the machine to retrieve his packet the cradle jammed fast in the opening.

In order to lever the finger free he used the gold razor blade which hangs on a chain around his neck. This managed to get jammed behind his finger.

When he tried to retrieve this, two of the rings on his other hand got jammed also, rendering him helpless.

He was there for some time before a customer came in to relieve himself. The customer reported to the landlord that someone was trying to eat the contents of the machine while they were still inside it.

The landlord, a kindly chap who will sometimes umpire for us, had one of the most raucous laughs you could ever wish to hear and when this noise came echoing from the Gents' we all decided to investigate.

To say that Al was red-faced would be the understatement of the year.

Our problem now, of course was how to extricate him. This was made worse by the fact that anyone who had to go would automatically dissolve into fits of laughter, and also by the fact that Al didn't want to damage his recent purchase.

Dick Dickinson went to his garage to get a miniature jack so as to prise open the small aperture but this proved too dangerous and nearly left Al with another broken finger.

Rather a lot of liquid soap was poured in to try and ease the hands out but this line of attack had to be abandoned because of the risk to Al's Gucci shoes.

In the end, with the start of play looming ever closer, it was decided to move the front of the machine. This having been done, it was found that a lot of the contents had been soiled with the liquid soap – which upset the landlord. (He did, however, put them to good use at a birthday party which was held in the Tap Room the following week.)

But Al was still stuck.

Well, we had to get to the game and you can imagine the comments of the opposition when we arrived with Al holding the front of the pubs prophylactic machine to his chest. If you looked at him from the front all you could see was a metal plate with fingers protruding from a hole at the bottom clutching a battered packet of three.

And this was the problem: Al refused to let go of them.

To save his blushes we threw an umpire's coat over his head and marched him into the dressing-room. The opposition thought that we had just made a citizen's arrest upon a sex maniac.

By this time we were beginning to think that Al would have to play like this. The metal plate could quite easily have been passed off as protective clothing (no pun intended) if we had him fielding at silly mid-off, but by no stretch of the imagination could it be passed off as a bat.

In the end, all was solved quite easily when Al was persuaded to let go of the packet and we understood why he had been so reluctant when we saw the shape and colour of the contents.

The upshot of all this was (again no pun intended) that when Al came to use them that night irreparable damage had been caused by the gold razor blade, so he couldn't use them anyway.

The metal plate that was the front of the machine was so battered during all this that it proved impossible to return it to its original position and now it stands with all our other treasures on the Tap Room wall.

The team we were playing that day were from a local branch of the Mormons known as the Latter Day Saints CC and all this activity had met with strong looks of disapproval.

Now in no way do I mean to be irreligious or disapproving of these people, but let's face it, one man's oyster is another man's whelk.

I must say that they were very good cricketers, but choruses of 'Praise the Lord' from an assembled multitude of women on the boundary after every shot got to be very monotonous indeed.

When a batsman was out it appeared to me that he had to go and ask forgiveness behind the dressing-rooms with some crew-cut pimply American youth in a sixties suit.

When one of them asked how many he'd scored and replied that he'd made 10, the youth interrupted and said that it was only 9 as 10 per cent of all earnings go to the Church. I think he was joking.

Then there was tea.

Well, not tea.

Not even coffee.

Not even Coca Cola.

More a kind of Lucozade concoction that had Mr Gloomburg with all his knowledge of drinks totally dumbfounded. It very nearly made me reach for Typhoon Turnbull's can of lager, until I realised that it was Australian and the taste wasn't much different.

Their disapproval continued as various containers of booze emerged along with packets of cigarettes. 'Do you mind if I eat while you smoke?' was one sarcastic comment.

However I must be fair and say that although I was dreading

the tea interval, because I thought it would amount to twenty minutes of them trying to convert us from our wicked ways, this was not the case at all and there was actually some quite enlightening discussion around the table.

This was all the more interesting when it was discovered that the basis of their religion revolved around the writings of some bloke who was killed in a Tap Room brawl out in the Wild West. This opened up all kinds of possibilities to Mr Gloomburg, who saw the potential of such a venture. But he couldn't decide which one of us to bump off.

Other misconceptions were cleared up and we actually had quite a pleasant day, especially when it was realised that all seven of the charming tea-ladies were not married to the captain.

Fingers Ashton, as if to celebrate this discovery, asked the ladies to come up with any female Christian name and he would come up with a song that included the name.

They came up with Norleen (which was much too Australian for my liking) and Fingers went into a trance-like posture of deep thought.

He then sang 'Happy Birthday' including the name at the end.

A crafty sod is Fingers and we all had a good laugh.

They won the game on the last ball and the bowler returned with them all for the evening service to give thanks for a safe delivery.

We thought it rather inappropriate to ask them back to the Tap Room afterwards for a quick pint.

I was reminded of the Reverend Lord Frederick Beauclerk who was the vicar of St Albans many years ago. Not only was he the son of Nell Gwynne and Charles II but around the Soho district of London, which he frequented often, he was known as Fred Diamond Eye. This man had an amazing disrespect for bowlers and would often hang a valuable gold watch from his stumps. He was also known as an incredibly boring preacher.

So Lucky, we hope your recovery is swift and if you think a

prayer might help, I'll send you the address of The Latter Day Saints CC.

Amen.

Steve.

9· *The Hollywood Doppelgangers XI*

16 March 1986

Dear Lucky,

One of our most recent treasures, now beautifully framed and placed on the Tap Room wall, is a page from last year's scorebook.

Here it is, copied out for you:

1. W. G. Grace	Bowled Turnbull	0
2. S. Stallone	Retired Hurt	0
3. E. Presley	Bowled Turnbull	6
4. G. Marx	Run out	3
5. H. Marx	Run out	0
6. M. Monroe	Hit wicket. Bowled Vet	69
7. C. Chaplin	Bowled Kildare	23
8. E. Flynn	Bowled Kildare	18
9. C. Eastwood	Caught and bowled Vet	23
10. M. Caine	Not out	29
11. H. Bogart	Caught Dave the Grave. Bowled Vet	10
	Extras	18
	Total	199

Now, after you've perused those names I'm sure you'll be wanting an explanation.

Yes, they really were W. G. Grace the cricketer, Sylvester Stallone the actor, Elvis Presley the singer etc., apart from the No. 10 which was Michael and not Marti Caine.

You may be thinking, 'How come this lot were lucky enough to get a game against the Ferret and Firkin CC, especially as most of them are dead?' Well, the answer is complicated, but bear with me.

A couple of months ago, Fingers Ashton was asked to provide the music for a television commercial which the Official Receiver gratefully accepted on his behalf. On hearing the news he promptly told Romeley S. Vet that auditions for parts in the commercial were soon to be held.

Ever ready to jump at any chance of fame, and thoroughly sick of 'resting', Romeley arranged an interview and went along, taking Fingers with him for moral support. The two of them trotted off to some seedy Soho office where they were shown into a smoke-filled room.

It happened that the producers had been delayed for over an hour, so when they entered there were some forty people all sitting around smoking Gauloise or biting their finger nails or comparing egos.

The point is that this commercial was employing an oft-used gimmick of using look-alikes of famous people – so when Fingers and Romeley entered they found themselves in the company of some of the most well-known people that had ever lived.

Now these two are both self-confessed 'groupies' when it comes to the famous; as a matter of fact, it is often said in the Tap Room if there is a loud crash of any description that one of them has just dropped a name. So, upon finding themselves in the presence of so many 'stars' they began to grovel unashamedly.

Eventually the conversation turned to cricket, which is their next best love after drinking, performing and grovelling, and it was found that many of the assembled also loved the game.

Especially W. G. Grace.

The outcome was an arranged charity match with the Ferret and Firkin.

The fixture was arranged and the look-alikes got a team together which they called The Hollywood Doppelgangers XI.

W. G. Grace apparently objected to the name as, of course,

he had had nothing to do with Hollywood. But he was appeased artistically when it was suggested that he could actually play C. Aubrey Smith pretending to be W. G.

It was the best role he'd had in years.

On the day of the game the teams gathered at the Ferret and Firkin amid great publicity and excitement.

It just so happened that the council were repairing the pavement outside the pub that particular week, so Mr Gloomburg, using his many contacts, persuaded the planning department to allow the stars to leave their footprints, handprints and autographs in the wet concrete.

Each star was introduced to a rather bemused South Hampstead crowd from a top window by Romeley who was revelling in reflected glory.

Flashbulbs flashed and many autographs were signed.

Dick Dickinson tried to get in on the act by pretending to be Al Jolson's little brother, but nobody took him too seriously, especially when he got stuck in the wet concrete.

We then adjourned to the Tap Room for a pre-match drink.

Errol Flynn escorted Marilyn Monroe inside, only to receive a sharp slap when he tried to find out whether she was wearing stockings or tights. It turned out that Miss Monroe was a female impersonator from Stepney called Geoffrey. Mr Flynn drowned his sorrows in a bottle of pre-match vodka.

Then there was an unseemly row between Mr Caine and Mr Stallone about football, each accusing the other of being totally useless. Mr Eastwood interrupted and said that although both of them had escaped to victory, neither of them had escaped from Alcatraz.

Things were getting a bit out of hand when the two Marx brothers began using the optics as a xylophone and Charlie Chaplin began running rings around Dave the Grave. When Typhoon Turnbull began to size up to Mr Stallone so as to see who was the real Rambo, we decided it was time to leave.

We arrived at our ground to great cheers from an assembled crowd. I must admit that I had done an excellent job in my capacity of Hon. PR Man and it was great to see so many turning out to watch the Ferret and Firkin.

This made me believe that we had at last arrived on the cricket scene proper.

I did have my work cut out for me for the rest of the day, however, as the stars seemed to be more interested in getting into photographs and signing autographs than getting on with the game.

The Hollywood Doppelgangers XI were put into bat. W. G. Grace obviously opened and he and Mr Stallone took to the field amidst great applause.

As they walked on, Mr Stallone was heard to say to W. G., 'Sir, do we get to win this time?'

'Straight bat, young man. Straight bat,' W. G. replied, fatherly.

Mr Gloomburg arranged the field as usual but thought it inappropriate to have Typhoon Turnbull open the bowling as this was a friendly occasion. The Aussie psychopath would have none of it, especially with the chance of bowling at Mr Stallone. He grabbed the ball and refused to let go of it.

W. G. Grace took his guard and Typhoon stormed in.

He Yorked him beautifully first ball.

An astonished W. G. looked up and said, 'Young man, they have come here to watch me bat, not to watch you bowl.' He then took his guard again.

Marilyn Monroe, the umpire, agreed and called a rather late, 'No ball'.

Typhoon was furious and returned to his mark.

His next ball was perfect: fast, pitching outside off and cutting in off the seam, sending the stumps flying for a second time.

Even W. G. had to bow down this time and he walked up to Typhoon offering his hand in admiration. 'Naff off you Pommy bastard,' gesticulated Typhoon, 'that makes up for my Great Granddaddy!'

Now this was news to us. It emerged that this relation of Typhoon's had been on the 1886 Tour and had suffered at the hands of W. G. in a way we were too afraid to enquire about.

W. G., however, left the field unruffled and to great applause.

Elvis then came in and took his mark as Typhoon returned to his.

As Typhoon ran up this time he quickly changed direction halfway to bowl around the wicket and crashed violently into Mr Stallone, who toppled to the ground, his leg quite badly lacerated due to the assortment of knives strapped there.

The General administered to his wounds and he was helped from the pitch shouting, 'Don't push me!'

Typhoon, meanwhile, was whooping around the ground shouting, 'There's only one Rambo! Only one Rambo!'

Marilyn Monroe, after calling another 'No ball', complained energetically, but coyly, to Mr Gloomburg – so much so that some of the padding fell out of her bra. Cronin the Librarian fielded the padding and tried to put it back. He must have been the only one who didn't realise that Marilyn was really a man.

Meanwhile, Mr Gloomburg remonstrated with Typhoon telling him to calm down and to behave himself.

As Groucho Marx came to the bowler's end, Miss Monroe left the field to pad up. As they passed he commented that he'd always known he'd been in the wrong movies and suggested that maybe they could make up for it later. She ignored him. He went to the wicket and Elvis took his guard.

Elvis was rather overweight but resplendent in his silk diamond encrusted whites and pads.

As Typhoon began his run up to what was officially only the second ball of the game, he was stopped midway by Groucho who produced a bottle of Bourbon and asked Typhoon if he had a can-opener. Typhoon stopped, smiled, rolled up his trouser leg and from a vast array of concealed weapons he produced one. Groucho refused, bit off the cork, spat it out and said, 'Thank you, but I'd rather have a bottle in front of me than a frontal lobotomy.'

Typhoon giggled like a child and, after lighting Groucho's cigar, returned to bowl again. (It turned out that he couldn't possibly be offended by the man as he reminded him of his mother.)

This time the ball was gentler, being due either to Mr

Gloomburg's words or the presence of Groucho. It was a slow full toss and was guided delicately away through slips for four.

Elvis turned to Fingers Ashton and called, 'Knock, knock.'

'Who's there?' obliged Fingers.

'Wurlitzer.'

'Wurlitzer who?'

> Wurlitzer one to the body, through slips for four,
> Now I'm gettin' ready to go man go.
> Now don't you, step on my new white shoes,
> You can do anything,
> But don't step on my new white shoes.

He sang, adopting that familiar stance and using his bat as a guitar even though he had a real one strapped to his back.

As he performed, the fielders behind him began dancing and clapping in time, a backing group in whites, finishing to thunderous applause from the crowd.

Meanwhile Groucho was unsuccessfully trying to strike up a conversation with Cronin the Librarian at mid-off. 'Tell me,' asked Groucho, 'do you think there's life before death?'

'Ugh,' said Cronin.

The next ball was dispatched for an easy 2. The two batsmen ran down the wicket quite distinctively.

As they passed the first time Groucho said, 'What do you get if you cross a tortoise with a vibrator?'

'Dunno,' Elvis called back.

As they passed for the second time Groucho told him. 'An armadildo.'

The next two balls passed down leg side quite harmlessly. This was due to a series of 'koochy-koos' from Groucho as Typhoon bowled, which totally destroyed his concentration and left him in fits of giggles.

This also suited Elvis who could concentrate on getting his quiff back together.

Coming in for the last ball of the over Typhoon was helpless with laughter and the ball dribbled down the pitch. Elvis was still busy with his quiff. The ball only just reached the stumps and the bails delicately fell to the ground.

As he retired, Elvis could be heard singing, 'You hit my sticks, but then I scored 6.'

'You should be on the stage,' called Groucho after him. 'There's one leaving in five minutes.'

As Harpo Marx came in to bat, the Hollywood Doppelgangers XI were 8 for 2 with one batsman retired hurt.

Only one over had been bowled.

Oh Lucky, if only you could have been there at this most bizarre cricket game.

Typhoon Turnbull had to be retired from bowling. The Australian was helpless with laughter, the tears streaming down his face. He was sent to deep fine leg where he rolled on the ground holding his ribs. It was all very astonishing to the rest of us as nobody had ever seen him smile before.

Romeley S. Vet opened the bowling from the other end.

It was a great occasion for him. This was his finest moment since appearing on *Emmerdale Farm*. And he revelled in it. The first man in history to bowl, medium pace, at two of the Marx Brothers.

When Harpo came in it was obvious that he had no bat and he searched through his coat looking for it.

Groucho approached. 'Where's your bat?' he asked. Harpo produced the famous car hooter.

'Honk-honk,' he replied.

'What do you mean it's in the belfrey? I thought your mother-in-law lived there?'

'Honk, whistle, honk-honk.'

'Oh, you're talking about your mother-in-law.'

Groucho was happy and he returned to his crease where he hung a 'Do Not Disturb' sign over his stumps. He took his stance and Romeley bowled, Groucho dispatched it, the timing immaculate as always.

As the two brothers met in the middle they stopped and followed each other around in a tight circle. Typhoon Turnbull could be heard screaming on the boundary as Groucho asked, 'Do you come here often?'

'Honk-honk,' replied Harpo.

'What a shame,' said Groucho, 'we need the runs.' And off they went for an easy single which should have been three.

Harpo took his stance as the ball was returned. He still had no bat.

'What guard do you want?' asked Clint Eastwood through gritted teeth and cigar.

'Honk-honk,' replied Harpo, stamping his foot down as though his leg were the bat.

'Erm . . . middle and leg,' said Clint. 'Right a bit . . . that's it.' Then he turned to Romeley who was standing wondering what to do.

'Well punk? Do you feel lucky?'

Romeley rose to the bait and stormed in towards a quivering, whistling Harpo Marx.

At the last moment Harpo produced a baseball bat from under his coat and cracked the ball away expertly. He then threw his bat to the ground and set off at a canter. Meeting in the middle, the brothers began to circle again.

'I thought you said you didn't come here often,' said Groucho.

'Honk-honk, wolf-whistle,' replied Harpo.

'I didn't know it was the mating season,' confessed Groucho and he sped off in totally the wrong direction, dangerously close to being run out.

Clint Eastwood tried to signal 'Incomplete Run' but his poncho got in the way.

'Haven't had so much fun since my last day at the races,' Groucho told Clint.

Romeley came in to bowl again but was stopped by a wildly gesticulating Harpo who was pointing to Charlie Chaplin on the boundary.

'What's wrong?' asked Romeley, as Harpo hooted.

'He wants that man to move the sight-screen,' said Groucho.

'What sight-screen?' asked an incredulous Romeley, as there weren't any on the ground.

'Jesus punk,' said Clint, 'are you blind?'

He and Groucho then went to the boundary where they

helped Charlie Chaplin to move the imaginary sight-screen to the loudly whistled directions of Harpo. When he was happy, they returned and the game continued.

Romeley gamely threw up another full toss which was cracked away again.

When the brothers met in the middle this time they crossed, but Harpo immediately doubled back and followed Groucho to his end where he gave him a rubber chicken.

'Lunch,' said Groucho, producing his bottle of Bourbon and a tablecloth as Harpo was run out. They then sat down, filled up the rest of the tablecloth with items of food and toasted each other.

In the distance, Typhoon Turnbull screamed uncontrollably.

When Marilyn Monroe came in to bat, Harpo refused to leave the field, insisting that it was Groucho who was really out. Groucho said that he had to be joking and moved in on Marilyn.

'What's a nice girl like you doing in a dump like this?' he asked, flicking cigar ash all over the wicket.

'Trying to get runs, you pillock!' said Marilyn, or rather, Geoffrey.

'This is going to be tougher than I thought,' admitted Groucho.

After Harpo had been escorted from the field at the point of Mr Eastwood's Magnum revolver, the game continued.

Miss Monroe, dressed in a white silk dress familiar to those who had seen *The Seven Year Itch*, plus pads and presumably a box, went on to perform an innings of sublime beauty.

Mr Gloomburg changed bowlers as frequently as possible but each one was firmly dealt with at the hands of Miss Monroe in a great exhibition of batting skill. It was reminiscent of David Gower at his most graceful. She went on to score a marvellous 69 and was disappointingly out, hit wicket, after she attempted a hook shot and her wig fell on to the stumps.

In the meantime she shared a succession of partners.

Groucho was run out after stopping to answer a phone call from his shoe halfway through a quick single. He was most disappointed. It was a wrong number.

Charlie Chaplin was bowled by Sean Kildare's accurate spin, though it must be admitted that he was disadvantaged by his decision to use his walking stick as a bat. He did, however, manage somehow to score 23.

Errol Flynn looked more like his old swashbuckling self when batting with Miss Monroe. When she was out, however, the heart went out of him and he consoled himself with a bottle provided by Groucho, who had returned to umpire. He too was out to Dr Kildare after playing the most drunken stroke I've ever had the misfortune to witness, even with all my experiences of drunken cricketers. But with great panache and a smile that had the ladies wilting he left the field to a very warm reception.

Next, Mr Eastwood and Mr Caine put on a very fine partnership amassing over 50 runs between them. There was apparently a bet between them to see who could make the most runs (in my opinion it was to see who could run the other out).

In the end, Romeley had Clint caught and bowled. To be exact, it was Mr Caine who caught it and tossed the ball slowly up into the air for Romeley to make one of his famous diving catches.

Romeley was so proud. There are not many people who manage to catch Clint Eastwood out and he proudly signalled this to his agent who was watching.

Finally it was the turn of Humphrey Bogart, who was warmly greeted on to the field, especially by Dick Dickinson who believed that *The African Queen* was a film about an ancestor of his (he wouldn't say whether the ancestor was male or female). When he and Dave the Grave went up to Mr Bogart as he walked on, with their autograph books, he merely looked up to the heavens.

'Of all the cricket games on all the cricket grounds in all the world, I had to walk into this one,' he cursed.

The first ball he faced was hooked beautifully away for the only six of the innings. 'Here's hooking at you kid,' he said to Romeley before putting the next away for four. He would have done the same with the next had it not been for an absolutely superb diving catch from Dave the Grave.

No one had ever seen him move so fast. We believe it was because he wanted to impress the man but in the end he was almost tearfully apologetic. He went up to him saying, 'Nyer . . . nyer . . .'

Humphrey handed him a handkerchief and said, 'This is your game Sam. Play it.' Then he and Michael Caine left the field to the most wonderful applause.

The Hollywood Doppelgangers XI were all out for 199 which by any standards was a superb effort. By theirs it was a bloody miracle.

Tea was a grand occasion – a glorified picnic in superb style, befitting to our distinguished guests – Irish linen tablecloths, silver cutlery, bone china, a candelabra and drink of every description served in lead crystal Tupperware

Charlie Chaplin did a charming little routine for the kids with two forks and two bread rolls and Marilyn Monroe asked who the President was as she fancied having an affair. We all pointed to Big Al who at first appeared interested and then blushed deeply.

But soon it was back to work and the Hollywood Doppelgangers XI took to the field.

As Mr Gloomburg and Sean Kildare went in to open the innings, there seemed to be some confusion among the opposition. It appeared that everyone wanted to get into the limelight by opening the bowling, except Mr Stallone whom the General had treated well enough for him to keep wicket.

There was plenty of threatening and finger-wagging from the tough guys and much gesticulating and honking from the comedians while Miss Monroe simply made do with certain promises.

W. G. Grace, the captain, sorted it all out by taking the ball himself while promising that everyone would have a go. He then remonstrated with Groucho for smoking his cigar on the field. 'It's perfectly all right,' Groucho explained, 'I don't inhale.'

Now, I don't know how studied W. G. was of the real W.

G. Grace's action, but in his first over he was tonked for 19. (It was an interesting talking point later that, if his action was accurate, then a hundred years ago most of the Ferret and Firkin CC would have got a place on the England side.)

Of course, he wasn't helped much by the fielding of certain of his team members. Charlie Chaplin tried to stop everything that came his way with the end of his stick and then played a little game of hockey. Groucho, on the other hand, simply stopped the ball dead then lay down to tell it a joke.

The tough guys appeared to be taking the game a little more seriously, apart from Mr Eastwood who kept taking pot shots at the ball with his Magnum revolver.

The following over was much better.

Charlie Chaplin was the bowler and he set a most extraordinary field. He put everybody, including the wicket keeper, at deep third man which was where most of the spectators were nearest. The stars loved this, apart from W. G. who strongly objected.

Charlie silently insisted, hooking his stick around his neck and dragging him off to join the rest who were already well into signing autographs or drinking.

Or both.

Charlie then measured his run up with his stick, got rid of some loose turf by using the stick as a snooker cue, stood up, took three quick swaggering steps towards the batsman, stopped, turned to face the umpire and chucked the ball over his shoulder.

It was a beautiful ball of perfect length which turned into one of the finest leg-breaks Mr Gloomburg had ever faced and very nearly beat him.

The next five balls were all different: one underarm, one underleg, one between legs, one lying on the ground and one very fast after an extraordinarily long run-up which began at square leg.

It was the first maiden of the game; it had Mr Gloomburg in all sorts of trouble and it was much enjoyed by all who were lucky enough to witness it. At the end, Charlie took a bow and walked quietly away into the distance.

After a long delay, caused by efforts to get the fielders back on to the field, W. G. bowled again. This over cost him 22 runs but he did manage to get the wicket of Sean Kildare.

This was a rather dubious LBW decision given by Typhoon Turnbull who was umpiring. Typhoon was laughing so hard at the antics of the two Marx brothers, both at mid-off, that it was thought that he gave the decision so that he could have a rest. He certainly got his wish because Mr Gloomburg replaced him with Dick Dickinson, much to the amusement of Harpo, who began feeding him peanuts.

Groucho said that he once had a girlfriend who was as small as Dick; in fact she was so small that she had to have wheels fitted to her earrings.

Charlie Chaplin returned for another superlative maiden over and then W. G. replaced himself with Errol Flynn.

Now this particular look-alike, though a wonderful person (I mean, I'm sure his mother loves him), was obviously an actor of the Method School and, while possessing the physical attributes of the great swashbuckler (well, maybe not all of them), did not possess his capacity for drink. After two very drunken attempts at bowling he retired to the dressing-room looking very poorly indeed. But there were plenty of young ladies willing to take good care of him.

He was replaced by Marilyn Monroe who, once she had removed her high heels, put on a fine display of medium-pace bowling to complement her lovely innings at the crease. Some of us thought afterwards that the reason she took so many wickets was because of the obvious distractions as she bounced towards us in that white silk dress. However, as she seemed to be the only serious cricketer in the side, she proceeded to take five wickets, the easiest being Big Al's who took no guard at all. He merely drooled, even though he knew she was really a feller. He was perfectly bowled, first ball.

However, while Miss Monroe was very tight, the bowling from the other end left an awful lot to be desired and runs were added quite quickly.

Harpo Marx presented us with some problems, but they were due mainly to the field he set. Everyone stood in a tight circle around the batsman holding hands while he bowled very high full tosses over the field. He then ran down the wicket honking and whistling in an attempt to catch the ball before it reached the batsman.

These were no ordinary cricket balls.

As a matter of fact, two of them were apples, one a bread roll, one a bunch of grapes and one a basketball which appeared miraculously from nowhere.

Harpo dismissed Typhoon Turnbull with an apple, which wasn't difficult as Typhoon was helplessly hysterical in the arms of Sylvester Stallone, the two of them apparently having made up their differences.

In the light of all these goings-on it was amazing that we scored any runs at all; but it was a day of surprises and great entertainment.

When Fingers Ashton came on for the last wicket we needed 57 to win. His partner was Romeley S. Vet, the other instigator of this 'cricket game'.

Now neither of these two have ever been known for their batting talents but they put on a superb display, both of them being totally in their element surrounded by so many famous people. They were helped by some incredibly bad bowling from Elvis who did himself no favours by refusing to remove the guitar strapped to his back.

Romeley's batting was especially delightful and we believe that one of the reasons was because his agent was watching.

Now this man had been very much involved in helping to set up the game (he even tried to get sponsorship from a cigarette company) and he had brought along a television producer. The agent was trying to get him to do a TV series about the 'Bodyline' tour from the English point of view. In other words he wanted it done properly. After watching this game though, the producer went away and put his money into a Ben Travers farce.

Meanwhile, Romeley was totally immersed in the character of a thirties Englishman playing for the Ashes; and soon he and Fingers had put on 56 of the 57 runs needed to win the game.

The scores were level and W. G. set a field to save the single and brought himself on to bowl.

The delivery was slow and high.

Romeley moved down the wicket to meet it. He took an almighty swing, sending the ball rocketing straight up into the air.

Then there was absolute chaos.

The whole field converged to take the catch. Everyone was calling wildly for it except Harpo who was honking wildly for it.

As they all converged they clattered dramatically into one another, limbs and bodies flailing everywhere, and the ball disappeared into the middle of the mêlée.

After they'd picked themselves up there were some heated arguments and accusations, which stopped only when someone enquired loudly about the whereabouts of the ball. Nobody seemed to know where it was or whether it had been caught or not but just as W. G. began to lose his temper there was heard a muffled honk.

Lying on the floor with a smug smile on his face was Harpo. And there, resting inside the car hooter, was the ball.

Immediately a great cry of, 'Howzat!' went up from the whole team.

And up went the finger of umpire Gloomburg.

Now though this was not technically a correct decision, Mr Gloomburg thought it the only fitting end to the game – the first tied game in the history of the Ferret and Firkin CC.

As the players left the field they were greeted with loud cheers and applause.

It had certainly been an unusual game.

W. G. said that this game would be remembered long after cricket ceases to be played.

'But not before,' added Groucho.

We returned to the Tap Room in great spirits. It had been a wonderful day and everyone intended to celebrate it fittingly – with one of Mr Gloomburg's special concoctions. He called it 'The Hollywood XI' as there were eleven different items in it and if you had too much of it, it would make your ribs hurt (as Typhoon could testify).

The landlady provided an evening meal which was unprecedented in Tap Room history – it was hot – and then Mr Gloomburg announced that over £500 had been raised for a local children's charity.

W. G. Grace then rose to give a not unfamiliar speech: 'Mr Chairman, I beg to thank you for the honour you have done me. I never saw better . . . boozing . . . than I saw today, and I hope to see as good wherever I go.' He then sat, or rather, fell down to appreciative applause.

The festivities went on well into the night with Fingers Ashton accompanying Elvis in some of his greatest songs and had many of us reminiscing tearfully and drunkenly about the days when we used to be Teddy Boys.

Oh Lucky, you would have been so proud of us that day.

The only sadness is that you were not there to see it or be part of it.

We did have an idea for including you. We thought that with all your bandages you could have appeared as the Invisible Man.

Take care, old friend, and good health from all the Tap Room.

Steve

10· *The Winds of the Typhoon*

22 March 1986

Dear Lucky,

What on earth are they feeding you in that hospital?

The letter I just received from you was almost illegible and just as unintelligible when it was legible. I will quote you the few bits I could read but they make no sense to me:

'The colostomy at square leg notches up the runs.'

'Shingles is coming in but must be out if mid-on can work all right to catch.'

'Had them in stitches in the covers but when the sight-screens were moved round they were all out.'

'The four slips were Ankle, Elbow, Chin and Coccyx with Bum in gulley.'

'Preparation. H. Piling in the runs at the nursery end.'

'Nurse should warm Bedserpan before putting in.'

Maybe you can translate them for me.

In the meantime, I will give you the benefit of the doubt and say that your medication is having a hallucinatory effect. Either that or you've written an amazing Absurdist poem.

If I were a religious man I'd say a prayer for you but apart from the occasional blasphemy when another Australian lager comes on to the market I tend to keep away from all that.

I now regard myself as a basic cricketing existential hedonist.

I believe, simply, that often you wonder why the hell you're so far down in the order and often you wonder why the hell you've been given out, but while you are in you might as well make the most of it and knock the shit out of the bowler at every chance you get.

Likely as not if you ever do get to meet the Great Umpire in the Sky, he'll probably tell you over a pint of real ale that he made a mistake and you probably didn't get a nick on it after all.

Sorry if all this is sounding overly philosophical but things haven't been going too well recently.

You see, I regard the game of cricket rather like a birdcage. There it is, all laid out, the theatre of play. The cage is the ground, the perch is the wicket, the cuttlefish the sight-screen, the mirror the changing-room, the water-bottle the bar, the feed tray the pavilion and so on, with that little bell announcing the start of play. And all the world can look in on you.

Trouble is, there's always some bird crapping all over it.

In the case of the Ferret and Firkin this bird has arrived in the form of Rayleen O'Connel, an Australian bruiser with all the charm of a mud wrestler and the subtlety of an air-raid. Even her name conjures up the flavour of her roots – that of man-made sterility based on Irish criminality. Rayleen is the bane of the Tap Room.

Not that many years ago, as you will remember, the Tap Room was, and quite rightly so in my opinion, a men-only bar. Women were not allowed to put a single foot in the place let alone pollute the air with French pongs and leave chewed lemon-peel in the ashtrays, but those days have gone. Since those halcyon days we have had the advent of the Pill and the advent of feminism which meant that you were forever getting your bum pinched when you went shopping on Hampstead High Street.

When the feminists arrived, the days of the men-only Tap Rooms were numbered.

The demonstrators outside our particular haven were horrendous and it took months to rid the place of the stench of burning bra-padding.

The landlord at the time decided to bow down to popular opinion – a decision which sent him to an early grave – and the doors were opened to the so-called 'fairer' sex. The first one through the door was Rayleen O'Connel, who caused Dick Dickinson to hide in the Gents' for three months. 'Stone me,' he said, 'it's bad enough being black!'

After two days most of us joined him there.

Now Rayleen, as I've said, is a big girl and frightening with it. Her sexual proclivities were legend in South Hampstead, which then had one of the highest number incidences of back trouble in the country. (Perhaps it was hereditary, as apparently her great grandmother was some kind of hostess on the *Titanic* and died when she went down on it.)

To Rayleen is accredited the story, now famous, of the taxi ride: on one of her first visits to the Tap Room she came in a taxi wearing merely a fur coat and a pair of moon-boots. On arriving she found that she had left her cash at home and the driver refused to take a cheque. After a slight row she smiled at the driver and opened wide her voluminous coat, probably made from the skins of several donkeys, to reveal her naked form. She then asked the man if that would do. 'Bugger me,' said the incredulous Cabbie, 'ain't you got anything smaller?'

When she first entered the portals of our beloved Tap Room we were lambasted with feminist tracts as she swilled down vast quantities of cooking lager and tapped her pipe against the laminated fireplace.

My introduction to her came when she interrupted a conversation I was having with Dave the Grave about the glories of the steam age. She was disgusted that there were not more women train-drivers.

'Nyer . . .' said Dave, 'you mean it's a woman's right to choo-choos?'

Rayleen spat in the fire.

The fire spat back.

If all this wasn't enough, Rayleen was rich. Her father had amassed a large fortune building a town outside Sydney which was based architecturally on the Butlin's camp at Bognor Regis. He had a speech impediment and named it after himself – twice.

It's called Woy Woy.

I have seen pictures of this place and looking at it I can see why it breeds the likes of Rayleen.

If the Great Umpire in the Sky should ever want to rid the world of herpes, AIDS, underarm bowling, cancer, the Chappell brothers, violent crime, Australian lager, Australian captaincy manuals, bank robbery, rainy Saturdays at the Lord's Test, beri-beri, Boy George, 'Bodyline' moaners and Kerry Packer, then all he has to do is give the world an enema and stick the end in Woy Woy.

While in London, Rayleen lived in a Hampstead mansion and often entertained visiting Antipodean luminaries and other feminists.

However, her behaviour changed dramatically with the arrival of Typhoon Turnbull. In him, for the first time after leaving Woy Woy, she had met her equal. His psychopathic energy and repulsiveness were the perfect match for her and she became a doting admirer.

He, in his turn, treated her with the respect he usually reserved for his dog, Satan, and often allowed her to change the oil in his Harley Davidson.

This transformation was as pleasing to us as it apparently was for her. Gone were the bone-crushing handshakes and the rib-cracking pats on the back along with the overpowering wafts of Chanel mixed with St Bruno.

Don't get me wrong, she didn't change that much, she could still be as forceful as ever, which is just what you'd expect from the girlfriend of a Hell's Angel. She was . . . well . . . let us say, a little subdued.

It was a perfect relationship.

She would sit there rabbiting away and Typhoon would smile, stoned out of his brains, appearing to listen, the occasional burp in response to a rare question.

After a while she was accepted into the Beelzebub Bashers of Botham as Typhoon's 'Old Woman'. She, in her turn, decided that he should move into her mansion. Up until now Typhoon had been living in a room which was rather reminiscent of a builder's skip, so he agreed and began to move the hundreds of motor bike parts he'd assembled there over the years.

However, there was one condition.

Of Typhoon's many disgusting and anti-social habits, the only one that was totally unacceptable to Rayleen was his penchant for raw garlic and baked beans. The man had an absolute obsession with them and while she could put up with the permanent smell of garlic, in no way could she put up with the flatulence brought on by his vast baked bean consumption.

It was a sticky point with them for some time but Typhoon resolved to give up 'the winds of Heinz' when his landlord threatened legal action after he'd driven away every other tenant from the house.

It was very hard going for him. He would often make pilgrimages to his favourite transport café where he would sit outside on his bike, moaning softly as he took in the aroma of baked beans. At one point he even tried hypnotism to rid him of his habit. That failed miserably when, in a deep sleep dreaming of baked beans, he ate the hypnotist's watch.

A year went by in which he never touched one baked bean. Rayleen was so proud of him that she forgave him any indiscretion – even sleeping with his bike – and on the morning of the anniversary of his kicking the habit she told him that she had a surprise in store for him that evening when he returned from his weekly 'rumble'.

When Typhoon arrived at the 'rumble' his heart wasn't in it.

Usually he would be crunching crash helmets with the best of them but he knew that it was exactly a year to the day since he had eaten any of his beloved baked beans and his stomach was churning. He left his fellow Beelzebub Bashers of Botham and drove frantically along the Hampshire country roads in noisy desperation.

Soon it was time to head home to find out the surprise that Rayleen had in store for him, so he stopped for petrol.

Alongside the petrol station was a roadside café with several bikes parked outside. Typhoon went over to inspect them and as he arrived he caught the unmistakable whiff of baked beans. Beans, glorious beans!

It was too much for him. He had to have a look.

As he stepped inside the café, six Hell's Angels from a Chapter known as The Satanic Slashers of Sight-Screens recognised him immediately and disappeared outside the back door leaving their half eaten meals behind. Each plate contained baked beans.

Typhoon sat down.

He prodded with a fork.

He said hello to each of them.

A tear trickled down his cheek.

Then he ate the lot.

Several extra portions later he was full and happy. Only when he reached South Hampstead did he realise that not only had he broken his promise, but Rayleen had her surprise in store.

As he arrived, shamefaced at Rayleen's door, she was there to meet him. She was enthusiastic, happy and very pleased to see him. Typhoon for his part was merely full of beans.

And his stomach was making strange noises.

She thanked him for being on time and prepared him for her big surprise. She took him into the hallway and blindfolded him. Then she led him into the dining room and sat him down at the table.

'My dear little koala,' she cooed, 'it has been a year to the day that you unselfishly sacrificed something very dear to your heart so that you could be with me. And just to show you how grateful I am, I have arranged this little . . .'

Just then the telephone rang.

'Sod it,' she purred. 'won't be a minute possum,' and off she lumbered to answer it.

By this time Typhoon's stomach was making very uncomfortbale though not unfamiliar movements.

He sat blindfolded and burped loudly.

Lower down the flatulence was becoming unbearable.

He listened; Rayleen was in deep conversation with someone.

He relieved the pressure.

'Fumf.' That was better, but there was more.

'Frumff.' It was becoming more uncomfortable.

'Ffrrapff.' Better. But still more.

'Fffrrroopff!' And smelly.

He reached forward blindly and found a napkin. He wafted it in front of him. But worse was to come.

'Brrraa-pa-brapa. Pimph!' More wafting. His dog Satan hid in a corner.

'GRREFFFA-FLAARRTER-RRHAAAMPFF!!' The cutlery rattled against glasses. This was ridiculous and he frantically wafted the all-too-familiar smell away.

Satan whimpered before an almighty 'BROOOMBEGARTLE-FLURBLE-FUMPFFF!!!' echoed round the room. The chandelier rattled and the windows shook.

Satan was sick.

Then he heard Rayleen replace the reciever.

He wafted fast and furiously for the last time. She entered and stopped. A look came into her eye. Then quickly and imperceptibly it spread to the other eye, but she chose to ignore it.

'Platypus,' she crooned as Typhoon sweated under the strain of holding it in. 'You've been so good this last year for abstaining from . . . you know what, that I've arranged this little reward for you. Darling wallaby . . . SURPRISE!!'

With that she whipped off the blindfold and there in front of him was . . . what? You've guessed it . . .

Twelve dinner guests.

Including her father, Woy.

Plus several Australia House officials.

And their wives.

And Rayleen's mother.

In the ensuing chaos Typhoon headed for the hills with Satan upwind of him.

As for Rayleen, she left the country the following day and hasn't been seen since.

That is until last week and this is why I'm not feeling too good. She has been away for ages and is now back in the vicinity with a vengeance, rather like Typhoon's wind. She has missed the re-formation of the Ferret and Firkin CC but has apparently returned demanding to be accepted into the ranks.

Demanding to play for us!

'Dick Dickinson is back hiding in the toilet. 'Stone me,' he said, 'it's bad enough being short.'

Typhoon appears to be cowering in a corner.

Mr Gloomburg is checking amongst his contacts at the Home Office to see if there isn't a way of getting her deported. But that will take time, and anyway he's very busy at the moment trying to stop a Chinese supermarket chain called Lee Fook from introducing an advertisement showing that they care about their customers. It has a picture of maternal Chinese eyes with a slogan underneath of, 'See, Lee Fook Cares'.

So we are dreading the arrival of Rayleen in the Tap Room

I will keep you posted. For now, take care,

Steve

P.S. Before I could post this letter to you Lucky, things happened.

Last night Rayleen hit South Hampstead.

Worse still, she hit the Tap Room.

All our Tap Room treasures had been removed from the walls and hidden in a loft for the duration. The optics had sticking plaster all over them to avoid shattering. The Gents' was being used as a shelter and a poker school had been set up there behind a score of sandbags.

At about 8.30 p.m. in she walked – the land leviathan.

If beauty is only skin deep then she was wearing her face inside out.

She wore a huge trenchcoat, polka-dotted wellies and Orson Welles designer jeans. If she was ever to hang a nightdress out to dry then I'm sure gypsies would camp in it.

'Who runs this puffy cricket team?' she announced, straight at me. As Hon. PR Man to the Ferret and Firkin CC I felt it my duty to reply, though at that moment I wished that I could play poker.

'I'm afraid, love . . .' I began, using my native Yorkshire accent to appear butch – well, butcher than her.

'Don't you "love" me, you sexist,' she interrupted.

Nothing could have been further from my mind.

'The secretary is not here,' I continued. I noticed that she had something moving on her shoulder. I found out later that it was her pet crab which she'd bought from an all-in wrestler. She called it Boston.

'Why are there no women playing for you?' she screamed, coming menacingly close to me.

'Well . . . er . . . the rules of the club . . .' I began, trembling. I would have explained the rules and told her that we played like a lot of old women anyway but I was interrupted again.

'Sheila!!'

It was loud and urgent and came from a dark recess of the Tap Room known as Crossword Corner. This is used by the drunker members of our company who find that they need to get a few down before they can get anything across.

'Sheila!!' The voice threatened again. 'Behave yourself!'

From out of the gloom stepped Typhoon, looking his most threatening, and he'd obviously changed over the years.

'Rambo!' gasped Rayleen. 'Is it really you?'

'Grrrr!' said Typhoon.

They disappeared together into the depths of Crossword Corner. Snippets of conversation could be heard. Typhoon was quoting Mr Gloomburg on the glories of cricket. Rayleen was gurgling.

Later they left the Tap Room, Typhoon leading the way followed by Satan, Rayleen and Boston.

I went to give the news to the poker school. They were playing 'Happy Families'. We all celebrated with Mr Gloomburg's latest concoction. It was a mixture of Irish whiskey and Chinese rice wine and was known as 'Shamwock'.

Later on I realised why women were not allowed within men's teams. In a game as noble and dignified as ours it would be quite unfair to subject the likes of Rayleen on anyone.
Except perhaps, a team of Aussies.
Good Health old friend,

Steve

P.P.S. Have you tried to spell the sound of a fart?

11· Teas, a Swearbox and Dick Dickinson

10 April 1986

Dear Lucky,

By the Lord Polo old friend, however did you come to have a washer in your pyjama pocket? I can understand that with all those weeks you spent in the children's ward you could have picked up the odd bit of Meccano, but that was some time ago.

But then to leave it in your jim-jam pocket when you're going for a chest X-ray – really! That's not just careless, it's downright criminal.

Sometimes Lucky I despair for you, I really do. Is it any surprise at all that they thought you had a hole in your heart? You of all people should know what these trainee doctors are like and if you don't you've only to ask the General. We were hoping that you'd be out soon but now I understand that it's yet more treatment for shock.

Soon, oh Lord's, soon.

Life in the Tap Room has been very slow of late. To be honest it's been bloody boring.

We've even had to do without Mr Gloomburg's concoctions as he's away on a short trip to America where he's doing some top secret advertising consultancy thingy. But he should be back soon.

He did ring through to the Tap Room and spoke to the General. He said that there was plenty of work for him and quoted something that was on television there to prove it. It went: 'This presentation was made possible by the Napalm

DICK DICKINSON

Corporation. Defending our heritage without nuclear weapons.'

Thank Lord's the Yanks don't play cricket or we could have lost our mentor forever. (As a matter of fact, I've often heard it said that the rules of the game were devised that way in order to make sure that the Yanks couldn't understand them and therefore would never play it.)

Unfortunately the General didn't get a concoction from him. It could have livened things up a bit.

Well, eventually over the last season we did manage to sort out the problem of teas. We've had many a pain with them I can tell you.

In the beginning we had a local of ours provide them. He is known as Harry the Greek and he runs a sandwich stall somewhere in the City. But we had to drop him in the end; we began to get sick of taramasalata and humus in pitta bread. The Doner kebabs could have been nice if hot, but cold – yuk!

After Harry we tried the system where everybody brings a little something. Unfortunately it was totally unorganised and we ended up with eleven varieties of Mr Kipling cakes.

Then, several wives and girlfriends were tried (if you see what I mean).

First of all Romeley's girl had a go. He calls her Little S because she's a little snob but her meal was fabulous: vol-au-vents, *haute cuisine* etc. The trouble with that was that it cost a fortune just for the icing on the cherry gâteaux, let alone the rest.

Next, Mrs Dickinson had a try. That was a nice change. It was just fortunate that we were playing a West Indian team that day.

After her, Fingers's lady, Big S, made an effort which was fine; then Dave the Grave's lady, Tiny S (well, she is tiny at the side of him), followed by the landlady Enorm S (she and Big S are known as the Tap Room's four bouncers).

Enorm S proved to be the most successful as she was the only one who enjoyed it.

All was well until Big Al pinched her bum one day while

she was in the middle of a sardine sandwich. Actually she was quite flattered but the landlord had noticed and all hell broke loose. At one point I thought he was going to bar the whole team, which would have been as tragic as closing down the bars at Lord's.

Fortunately, common sense prevailed and all was forgiven when Big Al apologised profusely to both of them; though why he should have had to apologise to the landlord is beyond me – I suppose he must have been jealous. Sean Kildare said it was probably because his cook was goosed.

Our only problem now is that we can't provide actual tea. There just aren't the facilities on our ground. Most teams don't seem to mind though, as they're usually too drunk to notice. We just fill a plastic container with orange juice and are thankful for being without the problems of limescale.

Having sorted that out, we were faced with a further problem. Some of us – well, to be honest it was only me – were becoming a little concerned about the level of language that was being used on the cricket field. In the Tap Room, to a certain degree, it's expected and accepted, but on the field I felt that it was very demeaning to the team.

Especially when used in front of visiting ladies.

More especially when it was used in the presence of our lovely scorer, whom I have the greatest admiration and desire for, the lovely Jan. I used to be so embarrassed for her when a player would come off swearing foully at some terrible stroke or decision.

Then I read of the Reverend J. H. Parsons of Warwickshire, who used to carry a swear-box with him on to the field and would fine professionals 3*d*. for every blasphemy and 6*d*. if directed at an umpire. I thought this sounded like a great idea, so I suggested it to the committee and was allowed to try it out.

At the next game I informed everybody that 10p would be charged for every swearword uttered and immediately raised 50p at the announcement. In the dressing-room, as various pieces of equipment were found to be missing, a further £1.70 was added; another 30p when it looked as though it might rain and an extra £1.20 when it did rain.

Everybody settled back and had a drink or three while waiting for the rain to stop. I took 40p in the two hours of waiting from a very comfortable team and went on to take £2.10 when the rain did stop.

All the money was of course going into club funds and it's a shame that I couldn't have included the other teams as I would have made a fortune.

I was feeling very proud of myself for being instrumental in protecting the ears of the lovely Jan. So proud in fact, that when I went out to bat, after leaving the swearbox with Dick Dickinson, I felt as if I were her champion and went on to make my highest ever score of 68.

When I returned, feeling very proud of myself indeed, Dick handed me the swearbox. I noticed that there was a cheque folded up inside it, so I asked Dick whose it was.

'It's Jan's,' said Dick to my unbelieving ears. 'She was a bit surprised at your batting.'

'Why a cheque?' I asked, in a state of shock, 'hasn't she got any money?'

'Oh, she's got money,' he gloated, 'just not enough, that's all. It's made out to the club for £6.80.' He then began laughing that awful high-pitched laugh which drives me mad.

I cursed him quite violently; an act which cost me 30p.

It had to be him to shatter my illusions – he's such a pain sometimes. Do you know, he actually believes that Brian Ferry is a ship that takes football commentators to European games? He really does annoy me.

He certainly did this time and I was thinking seriously of getting my own back on him by putting a wasp in his gloves or super-glue in his box, or something.

It's a long time since I had such a good sulk. It spoiled the whole day for me and I could hardly bring myself to look at the lovely Jan.

However, later that evening she told me that she'd done it on purpose to boost the club funds, which made me see her as lovelier than ever. And it was especially nice of her to refuse my offer of a lift home because it was out of my way and Big Al was going in her direction anyway.

What a kind and caring nature she has.

For some reason though I still had it in for Dick Dickinson, the creep, and I patted him on the head every chance I got. I even went to the piano to join Fingers Ashton where we sang songs aimed at him. Songs like, 'I'm looking under a four-leaf clover' and 'Climb every mushroom'.

We even made him sit on the mantelpiece to listen.

He's a funny bloke, is Dick. He's obviously got a complex about his height, or lack of it, and now he's getting one about going grey.

The mixture of Brylcreem and Grecian 2000 he slaps on his head can be quite repulsive at times. He's scared that if he goes totally grey he'll be mistaken for a pint of Guinness. But then, as the General says, there's nothing wrong with grey hair – just ask anyone who's bald.

His wife can be a bit odd too. Apparently they met when he first came to this country and his first job was working as a toilet attendant. She was working next door in the Ladies' and after a very short romance they were married. She's had it in for him ever since though, as she reckons he used her in order to stay in the country. I suppose she regards it as a marriage of convenience.

As I say, life is very dull at the moment as we can only dream of great deeds on the field and can't wait for the start of the new season.

But then life goes on. Any minute now, I'm sure.

I really don't know what to do with myself.

I think I may go up on to Primose Hill and count the pollen.

For now, old friend, good health.

Steve.

P.S. I realise after reading this letter that it may sound a little bit petty as regards Dick Dickinson – but then how would you feel about someone who backs down every time it comes to his round because he's short?

12· *The Ferret and Firkin CC's First Game at Lord's*

28 April 1986

Dear Lucky,

By the lords of St Bart's I've had very good reports about your new convalescent home. Apparently it's one of the best and all the signs now point to your being with us in the near future.

I'd like to complement your good news with some of my own but I haven't got any.

Instead I'll make do with the story of how the Ferret and Firkin CC played its first game at Lord's.

One thing I have often noticed about having a cricket team in this area of London is the inherent snob value of being situated so close to Lord's. The Tap Room itself is situated no more than a mile and a half away from Lord's but within this distance are a fair few pub cricket teams, all of them, merely because of their location, claiming the mantle of being pub cricket HQ. Of course, we at the Ferret and Firkin would dispute with any of them the legality of such claims.

We are, after all, the only club with such a Tap Room and that must put us streets ahead.

The trouble is, the closer you get to Lord's itself, the snobbier the teams become. Some would argue that this closeness is the only criterion, but I beg to differ. Lord's is situated in St John's Wood. St John's Wood was built by rich men to house their mistresses. So how can pub cricket HQ be situated in a defunct knocking-shop?

We might be mere pub cricketers, but we're not Australian pub cricketers, are we?

I rest my case.

However, it was with one such team that we contested the title on the sacred turf itself – well almost.

The argument began in the bar of the Lord's Indoor Cricket School. Mr Gloomburg and the General, in their wisdom, decided at the end of our first season that the close season should not be wasted and nets were arranged at the School.

To me it was a great honour and I boasted wildly to my Yorkshire relatives that I was the first of our line to take a wicket at Lord's.

The School itself is of modern, unpretentious design: a cross between a small aircraft hangar and a bowling alley. The trouble with it is that it's always very hot in there, which is hardly surprising when you consider the number of sweating bodies running up and down the place. Consequently, the small dressing-rooms, with an hourly turnover of nearly fifty persons, tend to be a bit on the smelly side, especially when the likes of Typhoon Turnbull leave their socks behind.

Certainly, after your net you always feel like a drink.

Or several.

After our first net we adjourned to the dressing-room for a shower.

Now every institution has a comedian, even Lord's, but I had the shock of my life when I found myself taking a shower with a blow-up doll. It reminded me of the time in the Headingley Members' Bar when a . . . but that's another story.

I removed the said doll from the shower and took it into the dressing-room, where we were greeted with much amusement and sarky comments.

Then, much to the approval of Dick Dickinson, the doll was adopted as the team mascot. We dressed her accordingly in a large white shirt with a club tie as a belt and went upstairs for a much-needed drink.

She was smuggled into the bar and was officially named Miss Summers after a maker's tag we found on her left buttock. (One of our company wanted to name her after his wife because she never kept her mouth shut either. But we thought it imprudent.)

It was a lively evening which included a very interesting conversation with one of the School's coaches, who had been asked to coach on a feature film about 'Bodyline'. He turned it down when he heard the rumour that Dustin Hoffman was to play Jardine.

But then an argument erupted about the ownership of Miss Summers with a St John's Wood pub team. The argument progressed into who were the rightful claimants to the title of pub cricket HQ.

In the end, after much drinking, including a Mr Gloomburg concoction of kirsch, gin and bitter ('KGB' – there were a lot of spy scandals in the news at the time), it was decided to play for the title on the sacred ground itself – a mere 100 yards away. Miss Summers was to be the prize.

It was lovely to see the ground illuminated in the soft moonlight. we could pick out the venerated New Tavern Stand Bar where in the 1985 One-day International Alan Border had smashed a six right into the waiting hands of Cronin the Librarian. The pillock had dropped it and it was months before we could find it in ourselves to forgive him.

Now, drunk as we all were, it was felt inappropriate to use the actual pitch itself – the George Davis incident was still fresh in our minds – so we set up a 'pitch' between the stands which were being dismantled.

(Mr Getty's stand cost a reputed £1.5 million and he was to become a Member 'in the usual way'. If he should require membership of the Ferret and Firkin CC I'm sure we could work out decent terms 'in the usual way'.)

We were doing rather well at 45 without loss when we were quite rudely chased off by security guards.

We retired to the Lord's Tavern where the issue was taken up again.

The opposition drove there in a variety of very expensive cars. They had all the trappings of snobs and their captain, a double-barrelled pillock of the first order, got very swanky about his Porsche.

Inside the Tavern we all sat at a table adjoined to one where two delightful young ladies were sitting. As the arguments raged they were asked their opinions and it turned out that they both worked at Lord's as secretaries. This obviously lent weight to whatever they said.

Various methods of resolving the dispute were discussed, a game for the moment being out of the question. All the ideas were either stupid, long-winded or downright petty.

In the end, Double-Barrelled was relieving himself (in the Gents') when he was joined by Mr Gloomburg and they began to talk about the two girls.

Now it must be said, and I mean no disrespect to them, that these girls did look, how shall we say, 'available', and it was decided that the winner of the argument would be the first team to have a member arrange a dinner date with either of them.

Mr Gloomburg announced this quietly to us and then, quite gentlemanly, allowed the opposition to have the first attempt.

Double-Barrelled moved in and we could hear snippets of talk, mainly about his Porsche and his business and his large St John's Wood house. A time limit had been set and when it ran out he retired, disgusted with himself, or the girls, having got absolutely nowhere.

Now Mr Gloomburg is nobody's fool. When he suggested the idea he knew quite well that we had in our company none other than Big Al, the maestro himself. So Big Al sidled over and struck up an intimate conversation.

Well within the time allowed he was walking out of the Tavern with a girl on either arm.

Double-Barrelled looked on amazed. 'What have you got that I haven't?' he shouted at Al as he left.

Al turned, smiled and looked from one delighted girl to the other and simply replied, 'Two.' Then they left.

Double-Barrelled was furious and moaned belligerently, having lost not only the title, but quite a lot of pride as well.

As we rose to leave he was still carrying on. Mr Gloomburg hushed him and then told him a parable. It went like this:

'There was once a mouse driving his Porsche through the

jungle when he came upon a large pit. At the bottom of the pit was a bull elephant which was trapped. The mouse kindly offered his services and using his Porsche he was able to pull the bull elephant out of the pit. The elephant was eternally grateful and promised that if ever he had the chance to return the favour he would only be too happy. Well, sure enough, a week later the elephant came across the mouse who was trapped in the pit and he was most grateful to be able to return the service. He strode across the pit and lowered his John Thomas to the mouse who scrambled aboard and was lifted to safety.'

'Well,' said Double-Barrelled, 'what's the point?'

'The moral of the story is,' concluded Mr Gloomburg almost gloatingly, 'if you've got a big John Thomas, you don't need a Porsche.'

We then left very quickly.

Only when we arrived back at the Tap Room and were recounting the night's events did we realise that we'd left Miss Summers sitting on the stand at Lord's.

'It's a shame that the Australians aren't playing tomorrow,' said an amused Romeley S. Vet, 'she may have given MacDermott something to smile about.'

For now, cheers from the Tap Room,

Hope to see you soon,

Steve.

13· Dave the Grave and the Ouija Board

10 May 1986

Dear Lucky,

By the Lord Death! I've had one of the most frightening times of my life. I thought I was a gonner – I really did.

With the exception of facing Typhoon Turnbull's bowling, what I've just gone through rates as the best laxative ever.

It all began a few nights ago when Dave the Grave brought a Ouija board into the Tap Room. I don't know what you think about those things but I for one will certainly have nothing to do with them again.

I must admit though, that I was very intrigued when it arrived. We all were. We even joked about it.

The General thought it was great as he hoped to be able to contact his wife, whom he said had been as dead as a doornail since the honeymoon.

Someone said we might be able to contact MacDermott because he's obviously dead somewhere – the Aussies have got a robot in his place.

Dick Dickinson said that he had a seven-foot ancestor that he'd heard about and would like to ask him what went wrong. (He also said that the word 'Ouija' derived from backwoods Jive talk and meant marijuana. But we doubted this – Dick has never been high in his life.)

We all gathered around a Tap Room table and four of us placed a finger each on a small glass on the board. It all appeared very silly but I became fascinated as the glass began to move around, apparently on its own. There were great cries to the effect that someone was pushing it, so the participants were made to swear an oath over the Tap Room wall treasures that this wasn't the case.

We then began again.

Dave the Grave took charge and asked, rather predictably, if there was anybody there.

The glass moved around the board and came to stop over the word 'Yes', which gave less cause for concern than if it had landed on 'No'.

Dave then asked the spirit's name. The glass hovered around uncertainly and spelt out, 'D-I-N-E'.

'It's hungry,' said Fingers Ashton, totally bemused by the goings-on.

It then spelt, 'J-A-R'.

'He wants a pint as well.'

Then, 'D-I-N'.

'It's a French gardener,' said someone, 'you know, Jardin.'

'Nyer . . . NO!' Announced Dave the Grave, 'It's Jardine!'

A gasp of shock echoed around the Tap Room. Some of us even stopped drinking. If this really was Jardine the possibilities were endless. Think of the questions that could be answered, the arguments that could be resolved, the valuable contributions that could be made to cricketing history. All those niggling doubts and uncertainties about Bodyline could be cleared up at a stroke.

So we asked away . . .

'During the 'Bodyline' tour of 1932–3, did the Australians have any decent lager?'

'D-O-N-T-B-E-S-I-L-L-Y,' came the reply.

'Is it true that 'Bodyline' was the trade name of a leotard that Bradman wore under his whites?'

'P-O-S-S-I-B-L-E,'

'What was Larwood's best performance?'

'T-W-E-L-V-E-P-I-N-T-S-I-N-A-D-E-L-A-I-D-E.'

'What do you think of Australian Tap Rooms?'

'P-A-S-S.' I'm fairly sure it was an 'A'.

'Is it true that you could only get real ale at the British High Commission?'

'P-I-L-L-O-C-K-S,' it spelt out – and then the glass broke.

We quickly fetched a new one but Jardine had gone.

All we could get was some idiot called Tinniswood who kept blathering on about Queen Victoria's pygmies going for Scarlet Rambles – or something.

We then adjourned for 'tea' which was a Mr Gloomburg concoction called 'Portergeist', a mixture of Guinness and Schnapps.

The General then told us of a house he'd once lived in which had the ghost of a cricketer haunting it. Apparently the General would throw bits of china etc. around the room and the ghost would catch them.

It was at this time that I told the story of my great-great-grandfather, Jobe Galloway. He was killed when the ball hit him over the heart – long before 'Bodyline' was fashionable.

Within the family there are a couple of heirlooms. One is a bat with an inscribed silver heart embedded in it. What it says, I don't know as it's hidden away in some great-uncle's attic. The other is a letter of condolence to my great-great-grandmother. Some great-aunt now owns this but it is signed by the great W. G. Grace himself – the proper one, not a Hollywood Doppelganger.

So, you can imagine my excitement when we returned to the Ouija board and the spirit spelt out its name: 'J-O-B-E'. My heart fluttered with all the anticipation one feels when a slow full toss floats towards you.

But it was at this point that I was struck with a searing pain in my shoulder – an old cricketing wound from my Boys' Brigade days.

Now I have met some pillocks in my time, but when Romeley S. Vet asked 'J-O-B-E' what the pain was, I thought him to be the biggest pillock of them all. Before I could protest the glass began to move around frantically and before my frightened eyes it spelt out the word 'C-A-N-C-E-R'.

I tried to call the whole thing off but the sadists persisted.

'When will he die?' some berk asked.

'T-W-O-D-A-Y-S,' said Jobe. I nearly fainted.

'How?'

'C-A-R.'

'Where?'

'B-R-A-D-M-A-N-S-T,' was all it said before I quite lost my temper.

Mr Gloomburg agreed with me and the board was packed away.

I was furious and it was only after several glasses of Portergeist that I managed to calm down. (I realised later why it had been given that name when it came back to haunt me.)

In the meantime an A–Z of London had been produced and everyone was busy looking for Bradman St. Fortunately it wasn't anywhere to be found. Nor a Road or a Square or a Drive or a Mews, or anything. It was interesting to see how the planners of London had remembered the great Aussie batsman.

The search was to carry on though and the next few days were quite nerve-racking. I tried not to take all this nonsense too seriously but on the following evening, the eve of my supposed death, I entered the Tap Room and found out who my friends were.

'Nice coat that,' remarked Fingers Ashton, feeling the cloth.

'Nyer . . . I always did like those pads of yours,' added Dave the Grave.

'Just getting used to your bar-stool,' said Romeley. 'I wonder what the lovely Jan will look like in black?'

'Have a drink,' said Mr Gloomburg. I thanked him and as he ordered he added, 'Have you made out a will yet?'

That was it.

I was fed up. My nerves were jangling and these people were loving every minute of it. I told them in no uncertain terms just where they could go.

They said they'd probably see me there tomorrow.

The next day was horrendous. I looked a dozen times before crossing any road, I kept away from any street beginning with 'B' and basically behaved like a man who had been given his last cigarette before the firing squad set to work.

Fortunately I met Sean Kildare who calmed me down

by telling me of the psychological motivations behind my nervousness and by buying me eight pints.

As we left the Tap Room I felt much better. I even shook a fist skyward at Great-great-granddad Jobe and sauntered out into the afternoon light not giving a damn.

The next thing I knew I was out in the middle of the road and there was a car horn blaring loudly.

I swung around to see a truck speeding towards me.

I dived.

I hit the pavement.

I scrambled across to the wall.

I shook.

The truck stopped and a man was shouting at me. I've no idea what he was saying. All I could do was stare at the advertisement on the truck's side.

It read: 'BRADMAN'S T-SHIRTS AND LEOTARDS'.

Then I was sick.

How I got home, I just don't know; but the rest of the night was awful. It was the first night in years that I hadn't been in the Tap Room. I didn't know what to do with myself. I certainly didn't fancy that night's horror movie on the telly. I sat and shivered under the duvet and when midnight arrived I was more than grateful it was all over.

Of course it's all a big joke now, but at the time . . .

Our latest acquisition to the Tap Room wall is a framed advertisement for Bradman's T-shirts and Leotards. It's hidden away in the dark recess of Crossword Corner. It sends a shiver down my spine every time I think of it. If I see it, it gives me a pain in the shoulder.

For now, old friend, cheers! I understand that we'll all be seeing you again quite soon. Looking forward to it.

Steve.

P.S. We had a quiz in the Tap Room last week. Here are a couple of the questions that had me stumped:

1. Who was the first English bowler to be knighted?
2. Who was the first Yorkshire captain to take a team to Australia?

Answers
1. Sir Francis Drake.
2. Captain Cook.

14· Lucky Returns

22 May 1986

Dear Lucky,

What can I say?

For you, if health and happiness were just around the corner you'd be living on the M1.

I wish there was something I could do to cheer you up, but this must rank as your final indignity. Look at it this way, Lucky: after this, things can only get better. There can't be anything else that can happen to you.

I am trying to look on the bright side of it all, and so must you.

For a start, it was absolutely wonderful to see you again after all this time. Really marvellous. And you looked so healthy.

I'm sure you could see just how much work had gone into welcoming you home. Everyone had chipped in and a great amount of effort had gone into the Tap Room decorations. The 'Welcome Home Lucky' banners took hours of dedicated work, as it is realised by all that you are, may I say it, the 'spiritual' founder of the Ferret and Firkin CC.

One can only say that what happened to you was a freak accident and everyone here has a great deal of sympathy for you. Witness, Lucky, the enthusiasm which greeted your decision to umpire for us. Believe me we were most grateful.

However, I'm sorry that the journey to the game was so long and arduous, but it was the only spare place left and we thought that the fresh air would do you good. After all, it's been so long since you travelled anywhere other than from one hospital to another. We really did think that you'd enjoy it.

As for the controversy surrounding your umpiring decisions, I for one have total sympathy with you. After all this time you can't be expected to remember everything and your eyesight can't be expected to be perfect after such infirmities.

Especially wearing an eye-patch.

A cricket team of such standing as the Ferret and Firkin should respect every decision of an umpire. That's what the game is all about.

I do blame myself somewhat for the accident.

Had I not been fielding where I was I could have warned you. I thought you were going over to talk to the horses.

The hospital you're in has a great reputation. It's a pity it's so far away as perhaps we could come to visit you more often.

But just look at it as another test you have to go through before returning to your former form.

If I may quote some encouraging words:

> Let Richards and Wood do what they may,
> Gooch will score and Gower win the day.

Yes indeed Lucky old mate, you WILL have your day.
For now, all best wishes from all your dear friends at the Tap Room. I assure you, you are greatly missed by all.

Steve.

22 May 1986

Dear Mr. Gloomburg,

I am writing to you in your official capacity as secretary to the Ferret and Firkin CC.

Never in all my summers of playing our noble game have I been so disgusted at the behaviour of a cricket team. Not even when the Australians adopted underarm bowling.

Whatever you or the rest of the team may think of my old friend Lucky, it must be remembered that he was the founder of the original Ferret and Firkin CC. As the team quite deliberately regard themselves as the 'gentlemen of pub cricket', to coin one of your own phrases, I would have thought that Lucky deserved better treatment, nay respect.

I would have thought that this would have been upholding the best traditions of the Club.

The Club thrives on such traditions. One has only to look along the Tap Room walls, festooned as they are with treasured souvenirs of our history, to see this.

It therefore pained me greatly to witness the attitude of some of our members when I announced that Lucky was to return. Comments like, 'Oh no, not that silly old fart,' may be appropriate when referring to certain Tap Room customers, but surely not to the Club's founder?

We all know the controversy surrounding his abandoning the club in the first place. His fits of pique and the burning of all his kit were all signs of a frustrated perfectionist, indeed a credit to the game.

Who could blame him? He would turn up every week to play with a team incapable of staggering out of the pub, let alone on to a cricket field. And the oft-quoted incident where he attacked his players with bat and pad must be seen in the light of his declining health (and in the light of their being all out for 7).

This is a proud man.

Attempting a petition to get him barred from the Tap Room was shameful. I had strong words with those concerned, and if you remember the last committee meeting it was agreed to welcome Lucky back.

Even so, I had to do all the decorations and 'Welcome Home Lucky' banners myself, totally at my own expense. That in itself should have been ample warning for me – but worse was to come.

When Lucky did arrive he looked absolutely dreadful; all that time in hospital had obviously taken its toll. What might have cheered him up or at least brought a little colour to his cheeks would have been a general hearty welcome. But it was sadly lacking.

I did my best but can you imagine just how embarrassing it is doing 'Three Cheers for Lucky' totally on your own?

Even after that, a few enquiries about his health might have eased the situation. The only thing vaguely like that was an enquiry from two of our company if he, with all his experience, could tell the difference between a lobster and a crab? When he replied, quite genially in my opinion, that a crab walked sideways, one of the two turned to the other and said, 'There you are, I told you that you were suffering from lobsters!'

This was not the welcome I had envisaged.

Was it any surprise then that I should make such a fool of myself by insisting that he should umpire for us, even though he obviously wasn't fit.

Of course, I had been so busy the previous days arranging things that I failed to notice that the fixture had been rearranged so far away.

Taking a man in Lucky's condition all the way to Warwick on such a damp day might have caused a dangerous relapse. When Typhoon Turnbull said that he would arrange transport for Lucky I was quite pleased that someone was taking an interest and left him to it. I had no idea that he was to take the poor man himself – and on the back of his Harley Davidson.

How he withstood the harrowing journey is beyond me and matters were not helped by you yourself offering him a concocted 'drink for the road' of brandy, cod-liver oil and

Benylin. Is it any surprise that he decorated the back of Typhoon's jacket so colourfully?

In the light of all this you can hardly blame him for such umpiring decisions. After all, it was a very cold day and the umpire's coat was still wet from the game the week before.

We all know that you can't be caught unless you've actually touched the ball but it's amazing that Lucky could see anything: he was floating so high from that concoction and still trembling from the journey.

Even so, after the fourth such decision it was appalling to see such disgraceful behaviour from our team members. No one saw me complain when I was given out LBW for a duck to a ball that pitched three feet outside leg stump.

If, as was suggested at the time, he was trying to get his own back on certain people, then I for one can hardly blame him.

What finally happened sickened me.

When a man in his condition needs to relieve himself then every courtesy should be shown. From my position on the opposite boundary it at first appeared that this was the case and the team were being very helpful.

I saw people pointing him in the direction of the horses.

I saw people pointing to where he should stop.

Only when it was too late did I realise that he had stopped in front of the electric wire which kept the horses off the pitch. I tried to stop him but I was too late.

It must be bad enough touching one of those things, let alone urinating on one.

The poor man's screams were pitiful. Even more sickening was the ensuing laughter from every member of both teams as he danced and rolled around the boundary.

In the light of this was it at all surprising that I should lose my temper? I was disgusted. But of course that does not excuse my behaviour with Typhoon who was laughing louder than most and shouting, 'Now wash your hands!'

It is true that in the ugliness that followed I did knee the Australian lunatic between the legs. I apologise to him and the committee profusely for such ungentlemanly behaviour on the cricket field, especially as he was on our team. However, you may like to know that my kneecap has been replaced and is now on the mend.

So, in the light of all these events, in the light of Lucky's continued internment in yet another hospital, I feel that I have no other recourse than to resign from my position as Hon. PR Man of the Ferret and Firkin CC.

Neither do I wish to be considered for the team again.

It saddens me greatly, but then not as much as the behaviour on the field that day.

I used to believe that our club was something special but now I realise that it's just another pub cricket team.

Yours sincerely,

S. J. Morley Esq.

P.S. I enclose Fingers Ashton's song which I borrowed to send to Lucky.

Somehow, at the moment I think it would be most inappropriate.

15· *The Song of the Tap Room by Fingers Ashton*

Cricket's such stuff as dreams are made on,
Heath Extension was the ground we played on.
All of us dreamed of the times that would be,
Forming the Ferret and Firkin CC.

The days they were cold as the winter was long,
Fingers the Singer would give us a song
To warm up our hearts. How happy were we
To play for the Ferret and Firkin CC.

The Jewel in the Crown Tandoori Restauraunt:
Terrible food but a nice enough haunt
To write down the very first team that would be
Playing for Ferret and Firkin CC

Chorus

Ferret, Ferret and Firkin CC.
It hurts in my arm and it hurts in my knee,
It hurts in my box and it's so hard to see
That wonderful Ferret and Firkin CC.

Our mentor was Gloomburg, a true proper gent,
Some of us thought that he was heaven sent
In making of drinks varied as can be
And warming the souls of the Tap Room CC.

The General was happy with tactics and wars
Could oft see the end but never the cause
And all of the time his advice was quite free,
Befitting his role as the Tap Room GP.

FINGERS ASHTON

Chorus

In case of a birth there was Dr Sean,
Curator of kit and of newly born,
Deliveries of course were nothing to he,
Maker of runs for the Tap Room CC.

Big Al was a man, you know what I mean,
Except with his hands inside a machine,
The girls always knew where Big Al would be,
Playing around in the Tap Room CC.

PR man was Steve, a serious man,
Madly in love with the loverly Jan.
When she was around there was nought he could see.
Trying to score in the Tap Room was he.

Chorus

Talking to Cronin could make your heart sink
You thought you were facing the Missing Link.
A hitter of balls, not much repartee,
Slogging for Ferret and Firkin CC.

Dickinson was a West Indian gnome,
Who thought he knew all there was to be known,
It's said that he got his Brylcreem for free –
The Ferret and Firkin mascot you see.

At six foot eleven there was Dave the Grave,
Who was never known to rant or to rave,
Nyer . . .' and then, 'Nyer . . .' was a sentence for he,
Knockin' 'em dead in the Tap Room CC.

Chorus

From Emmerdale Farm came Romeley S. Vet,
Actor of method, not quite made it yet.
He'd dive like a gull and jump like a flea,
Performances daily, South Hampstead, for free.

Turnbull the Typhoon was Rambo with wind,
Local Hell's Angel, in all things he sinned,
Especially eating baked beans for tea
And clearing the Ferret and Firkin CC.

Chorus

So here were the men, pub cricketers all,
Dreamers of dreams and hitters of ball.
Collectors of glory, the best you could see,
Festooning the walls of the Tap Room CC.

Destroyers of coolers, upholders of name,
The best that a pub can offer the game.
What more could a boozer expect to be
Than to play with the Ferret and Firkin CC.

So bring all your coolers and tubes to a game,
We're flying the flag, we're burning the flame
Of Tap Room pub cricket, the way it should be,
As playcd by the Ferret and Firkin CC.

Chorus

16· *Dear Steve*

W. G. Gloomburg Esq.,
c/o The Tap Room,
The Ferret and Firkin,
South Hampstead.

20 June 1986

Dear Steve,

It was with a feeling of deep regret that I read your letter of resignation from the post of Hon. PR Man to the Ferret and Firkin CC.

Your contributions to the side since its formation have been worthy and admirable. Since you've been gone there have been countless arguments as to who will carry the kit and the sandwiches and who will run the scoreboard during the game.

I understand totally your feelings about our team members as I witness these arguments and I appreciate more than ever the position you held within the team. That you always carried out these necessary tasks without complaint and without thanks is applaudable – and you must forgive me – for I along with the others took you damnably for granted.

All this has been a great eye-opener for me. All those months ago when I organised the team I treated the task like a crusade. It was a wonderful hobby for me – this organising of a body of men into a delicate machine – all for the glory of our noble and beloved game.

Do you remember the times when we would stand before a game, caps doffed, all facing in the direction of St John's Wood to recite our Lord's prayer? I think that was the highlight of it all for me: the bashing of the infidel.

But I realise now that it was just another game to the lads.

I was always in mind of – nay, I modelled myself on – Sir Pelham Warner, the manager of the 1932 Bodyline Tour. When they were on their way to Australia there was a bishop travelling on the liner with them and Sir Pelham asked if it was permissible to pray for victory. The Bishop asked to sleep on the question and at breakfast the next morning he gave his ruling: he said, 'Anything that conduces to the glory of England was a meet and fitting subject for prayer.' And England, of course, won the series.

Well, that was how I used to think. How stupid of me, as I was dealing not with a body of gentlemen cricketers but with a body of Tap Room piss artists.

The only saving grace (if you'll pardon the pun) was that for a while, at least, it worked. But in the end I felt as David Shepherd must have felt in Australia when, the day after a particularly bad day in the field, he baptised a baby in Melbourne. As the mother passed the baby over she pleaded, 'Please don't drop this one.'

But then I have learned so much since we dug out that old team photograph. I mean, I always used to think that Rambo was a French poet! And I actually believed Romeley – after all he is in the business – when he told me that Dolly Parton was the best female double-act around!

As they say, cricket is a great leveller. Tap Room cricket is the greatest leveller of all.

But still I'm very proud of this lot – delinquent as they are.

I look at our trophies on the Tap Room wall and my eyes mist over with pride. I can't help it. To me there is something glorious about that first team sheet, something splendid about the front of that prophylactic machine and something adorable about Julie the Club Jug. The XXXX collage of cooler pieces, of course, is my favourite.

So I admit my faults. I'm proud, nay, overproud, nay, pompous about my team. And I don't give a damn. When you do a job like I do it's great to be able to take something seriously.

I mean, you wouldn't believe the rubbish I have to put up

with at work. I sit in my office sometimes and think that although it's not exactly the end of the world, if you look out of the window you can just about see it. The spot I'm in I wouldn't give to a dry-cleaner.

I'm at present working on two jobs in my advertising business. Somehow I have to manage a campaign for a Greek washing-up liquid called 'Plato' and a Japanese supermarket chain called 'Tenko'. And Romeley S. Vet is trying to get me to produce a pantomime which is a cross between Peter Pan and Cinderella called 'Fly Buttons'.

I despair. I really do.

So, as you can see, I really need my Tap Room and my Ferret and Firkin CC. Life really would be meaningless without them.

And, Steve, I need you. I depend so much on you. I've only just realised, for example, that we've not yet had a cricket dinner. Had you been around I'm sure it would have been mentioned if not organised.

Please reconsider your resignation.

I promise you can bat No. 3.

I have lambasted the team for their behaviour towards your old friend Lucky, and apologise most sincerely for their, and my behaviour towards him. I myself did not know the man, but even if he did used to be, as they still maintain, 'a miserable old bugger', it was no way in which to treat a sick man.

I assure you that they are all now most suitably apologetic and we have sent him a rubber-lined cricket box which we thought would be a psychological boost to his recovery.

Please accept this letter as a formal invitation to the club dinner, which has now been arranged and, late as it is, will be held in the Tap Room in two weeks' time.

As I said earlier, you are sorely missed.

Yours, most sincerely,

W. G. Gloomburg.

17· *The Club Dinner*

6 July 1986

Dear Lucky,

I must immediately apologise for not writing earlier and for not keeping you informed as to the progress of the team.

To be honest I haven't been particularly involved with the team of late, due to my moving house, setting up a new business, some ill health, the loss of my wisdom teeth and a compound fracture caused after an evening in a pub whose beer I was most unfamiliar with.

As a matter of fact I've been on a bit of a beano of late, or, as they call it up north, 'on the razz'.

And quite frankly I don't give a damn – it's something one just has to do from time to time – and, as the General puts it, there are a lot more old drunkards than there are old doctors! (Actually it was Benjamin Franklin who said that but the General never quotes anybody other than Napoleon by name. Silly old sod – he was talking about his sex appeal the other day and was complaining that he hadn't had a single donation.)

But then my troubles fade into insignificance compared with yours.

I spent some time trying to find out where you were. I presumed that after all this time you would have left the last hospital you were in but it wasn't until I returned to the Tap Room that I discovered that you were still in the same place. I was at a loss as to the reason why and it was a long process of discovery before I found out.

Yet again you have my total sympathy.

The shock you received from that electrified fence to that

particular part of your anatomy must have been like a thunder-bolt – it was enough to put anyone in hospital (or horsepiddle if you'll pardon the pun). It brings tears to my eyes just thinking about it.

But then I was told that the end of your appendage was so singed that circumcision was necessary.

You poor old cock you.

But then circumcision's not such a bad thing really. I mean, the Jews have been practising it with alacrity for years, as Mr Gloomburg will testify. Indeed it was Mr Gloomburg himself who suggested that we turn this year's cricket dinner into a barmitzvah in your honour.

But I must admit that I thought it particularly cruel that your first meal after the operation was a plate of cockles and mussels. I do know what a strong imagination you have.

However, I thought it a lovely gesture of the lovely Jan to come and visit you and deliver the present from all the lads at the Tap Room (the rubber-lined protector).

I understand your feelings exactly.

I think I have told you before that I regard Jan as the perfection of womanhood. I have long admired her from afar. Her physical beauty, that wide-eyed look of innocence, the way she walks and her total bearing are perfectly matched by her ability as a scorer.

I have long looked upon her as my ideal of femininity.

I must say that I found it unusual that she was wearing such erotic clothing. The thought of her in a see-through blouse, a split mini-skirt and stockings has given me many a sleepless night since I was told of it.

I believe that she had been to a fancy dress party in the locality – one of those 'vicars and tarts' affairs – escorted by Big Al; can you just see him as a vicar?!

So I understand perfectly what happened. Let's face it, she'd turn me on if she was wearing a sack. (Exactly the opposite of Typhoon Turnbull's lady who I believe was built when meat was cheap.)

That you should get so excited is perfectly understandable,

being denied female company for as long as you have. After all, you're only human.

It's such a pity that you burst all the stitches. I understand that the mess was appalling.

(Is it true that when the doctor examined you he asked you, 'How long has it been like that?' and you replied, 'That's as long as it's ever been.'? I thought that was very witty of you, all things considered.)

Anyway Lucky, as I said, for various reasons I have been away from the Tap Room. When I did return I was overcome with nostalgia. The familiarity and warmth of the place as I stared at my first pint had me glowing with a wonderful sense of security.

And as my old cricketing/drinking companions greeted me I was quite overcome.

It made me reflect long and hard about all the other Tap Rooms in the world and about the nonsense of our licensing laws. How dare they throw us out of these places, which are more home than home to most of us. If this really is the age of free enterprise then they should have dormitories built alongside our Tap Rooms. By the Lord Tetley – wouldn't it be grand!

But now Lucky I can relate something which I know you'll be dying to hear of: the first ever Ferret and Firkin cricket club dinner.

Now as you know, July is not exactly the traditional time to hold your average cricket club dinner. That ours was then was due to some unfortunate oversight on the part of the pillock who should have remembered.

But be that as it may, the dinner was arranged for a particular Sunday afternoon after the day's game had been rearranged. The game, in fact was played the day before. It was my return to the side after my short absence. And what a fiasco it was.

We turned up on rather a wet Saturday at a pub which we were told was near to the ground. The General and Mr Gloomburg went out to find the ground and left us in the pub.

Dick Dickinson tagged along with them, the intention being that he should return to let us know what was happening.

What the hell happened, I don't know; but somehow the silly sod had got hold of the wrong end of the stick and returned to tell us that the game had been 'more or less abandoned'.

Well, this was fine by us. We had already struck up a good friendship with the landlord of this particularly interesting hostelry and he locked the doors with us still inside.

It was only after many a pint of rather nice bitter had found the mark that we noticed what a particularly nice day it had turned out to be.

Dick Dickinson decided to go and find out what had become of the General and our mentor Gloomburg. He came racing back and banged on every window in the pub to be allowed in. He then informed us that the game had gone ahead and the two of them were out there batting for all they were worth.

By the time we'd finished our drinks and staggered out into the beautiful sunshine and found the ground, what we saw was almost unbelievable.

The two of them were batting as if it had gone out of fashion against a not inconsiderable attack and field.

They had put on 214 without loss and were in the last over.

Gloomburg was 101 not out at the end and spent the rest of the day trying to convince one and all that the Ferret and Firkin CC was indeed blessed (well, if not, certainly jammy).

We went on to win the game after one of the most drunken displays of fielding you could ever be fortunate enough to see.

The other team were treating us with so much respect after this superb display of batting that they just played for the draw right from the start. And I'd love to tell you how we did it but I fell asleep in the outfield soon after the start.

So, to the club dinner, which took place the following day: the first ever Ferret and Firkin CC dinner – what a grand occasion it was.

Everyone was dressed in their best glad rags and all the team were wearing their Ferret and Firkin CC sweaters and

TYPHOON TURNBULL

ties. Most of the sweaters were immaculate, especially Big Al's which was made of silk, but Dick Dickinson's proved so big on him that it looked like a dress and he had to use his tie as a belt.

Dave the Grave's looked like a bib and Typhoon Turnbull's looked as if he'd been sleeping in it for a month – in actual fact he'd been using it to keep his motor bike warm at night. Even his girlfriend Rayleen was wearing one in which she'd pulled out some of the letters so that the logo spelt 'FEET AND KINC'. Either this was some particular fetish she was into at the time or it could have been an Australian love cry. (Come to think of it, I always thought the Australian love cry was 'Brace yourself Sheila, I'm coming in!'.) She'd also wrapped Typhoon's club tie around his dog Satan, and most odd it looked too.

The dinner was held – where else? – in the Tap Room itself, one Sunday afternoon when the pub had closed.

As the doors were locked there began a ritual which had apparently grown up during my short absence.

From one end of the bar one of our company sang out a loud, 'Hi, ho!' This was echoed by someone else from the other end of the bar, and one after another each member of the team took up the chant. At the same time they all fell to their knees and before long we had a troupe of dwarves walking around the Tap Room singing, 'Hi ho, Hi ho, it's off to work we go!' etc.

The lovely Jan stood on a chair and waved a silk handkerchief.

This ritual takes place now every time the team leaves to play a game: they all leave the pub on their knees – except of course, for Dick Dickinson who doesn't need to.

(A picture of Snow White and the Seven Dwarves is now on the wall as yet another Tap Room treasure.)

Another ritual which has grown up is the one called 'Rats!'.

Someone is appointed for the day as the Pied Piper and at any time he wishes during a session (and fortunately not on the field) he shouts, 'Rats!' Everyone, wherever they are, or whoever they are talking to, has to throw themselves suddenly on to the floor, on their backs, wiggling their arms and legs and squeaking like a rat. The last one to do so is immediately fined £5 which goes to the Julie the Team Jug fund.

As you can imagine, this can prove most embarrassing at times; but it has proved most useful for those jealous of Big Al when he's chatting up someone's wife or girlfriend. In the few weeks that it's been going I believe that Al has had to fork out £35.

So, as the food was being laid out around the Tap Room by the landlady and bar staff, these rituals were in full flow.

Fingers Ashton took to the piano and the General began to sing operatic hits – not helped by Ashton improvising in a rock rhythm.

It was just as well really. The only difference between the General and Enrico Caruso is that Caruso's been dead longer.

It was at this time that I fell victim to the three-man lift routine.

I was told that Cronin the Librarian had been working on this with help from the others for some time – i.e. the enormous task of lifting three men who are lying on the floor. Looking at Cronin I could well believe this to be entirely possible, so I enthusiastically joined in.

The build-up was magnificent, beautifully orchestrated by Dr Kildare who used all his Irish blarney to effect the true showman.

Everyone gathered around as three of us lay on the floor – myself in the middle with Typhoon Turnbull and Big Al on either side of me. We were told to link arms and legs – all my limbs being linked to two each of the men on either side.

In the meantime Cronin had stripped down to his string vest and was being massaged by Romeley and wafted with a bar towel by Dave the Grave.

I must admit that I was totally fascinated as to how Cronin could possibly lift the three of us as we were encouraged to cling to each other with greater strength. They let Cronin go and he moved us even closer together and took a position straddling our six legs.

He flexed his muscles, was given a final swig of his pint before letting out a huge neolithic roar.

He then bent down and unzipped my flies and undid my belt.

Of course, I was totally helpless as I struggled in vain – realising immediately I'd been had.

Quick as a flash Cronin was handed a soda syphon and my crotch was soaked.

The whole Tap Room dissolved in laughter but it took me some time to see the funny side of it – after all, this escapade had been witnessed by the lovely Jan herself. It must have been so embarrassing for her – indeed, as I cleaned myself up afterwards I caught a glimpse of her flushed face, a tear trickling down her cheek.

Then we settled down to eat.

The food provided by the landlady was an amalgam of every type of pub food you're ever likely to see. It was basically a simple spread and contained many of our favourite dishes. Two in particular were the Elephant Vibrators and the Lemming Meringue Pie.

The first dish was so named because it had originally gone up on the menu as 'Jumbo Bangers' and the second because every time you were served a piece of it, it threw itself off the plate.

There was also some rather nice pheasant which Dick Dickinson kept calling 'peasant'. Fingers Ashton told him that it wasn't really peasant but was in fact fartridge.

Typhoon Turnbull had his very own dinner which was a huge bowl of baked beans. His girlfriend Rayleen was keeping very quiet. As a matter of fact, she behaved admirably throughout, apart from one occasion when she got upset when offered a crab sandwich. Memories of her pet crab Boston were still in her mind: Boston had disappeared one weekend when she had been away and she returned to find nothing but a smile on the face of Satan.

As the meal progressed there were many interesting topics of conversation that I overheard.

One was the General giving a long description of the Charge of the Light Brigade after a question from Dave the Grave.

After he had finished Dave looked vacant and then asked, 'Nyer . . . what are you talking about?'

'The Crimean War,' replied the General.

'Nyer . . . what's that to do with my electricity bill?' asked Dave.

He's a terrible wind-up merchant at times is Dave.

Another snippet I overheard was Dick Dickinson insisting to Dr Kildare that genitalia were not what the doctor thought, but in fact were the people who worked for an Italian airline. The good doctor bowed to Dick's obviously superior knowledge – after all, with a name like that he must know much more about the subject than a mere gynaecologist.

Mr Gloomburg had concocted a new drink to celebrate his century the day before. It was thus far unnamed and he was trying it out on anyone brave enough to give it a try. Romeley S. Vet was ever willing and as they downed what must have been the seventh glassful they began to justify this excess with quotations.

'*Bibo, ergo sum*,' said Romeley, 'I drink, therefore I am.'

'I drink to make other people interesting,' came Mr B's reposte, 'spoken by George Jean Nathan.'

'Water reflects your image, wine your soul. An old Roman saying.'

'Beer that is not drunk has missed its vocation. Meyer Breslav.'

'A toast given by Humphrey Bogart after reading a Greek play: "Here's looking at Euclid."'

'Ambrose Bierce said that brandy is a cordial composed of one part thunder and lightning, one part remorse, two parts bloody murder, one part death-hell-and-the-grave, two parts clarified Satan and four parts Holy Moses! Ability to quote this got me my first job,' concluded Mr Gloomburg.

He then poured himself a large glassful of the revolting mixture they'd been trying out and staggered to his feet to deliver the first of this special day's speeches.

'My friends,' he began, very shakily holding on to Romeley's shoulder for support, 'Gentlemen . . . It has been a most wonderful year for me. And . . . I'd just like to say . . .' He paused, took a drink and then a painfully deep breath before holding his glass high. 'Cheers. Here's mud in your eye. Good health. Bottom's up. *Sláinte. Na vas zdravi. Egészse-gére. Nazdrave. Salud. Lechid da. Zivili. Prosit. Eis uyeian. Á votre santé. Salute. Gezond heid. Sihhatiniza. Nazdrowie. Sanatate. Na Sdorovie. Sláinte mhath. Sköl.*'

He then slid under the table.

Romeley tried to help him but was very nearly dragged under with him. He managed to stop himself by resting his chin on the table top. For most of the rest of the afternoon he stayed there, grinning stupidly, a grim testament to Mr Gloomburg's inventiveness – the head of the table.

It was left to the General to take over the speechmaking.

He began a really tedious speech comparing our team to Napoleon's Old Guard – faithful and trusting to the end.

Fingers Ashton spiked his drink when he wasn't looking with some of Mr Gloomburg's concoction. It had the desired effect.

The General stopped in mid-sentence, his mouth wide open, unable to speak. He sat down and stayed like that for the rest of the day.

Next Dave the Grave rose and began his speech. 'Nyer . . . Nyer . . . Nyer . . . Nyer . . .' he began, obviously overcome with nerves. All that probably summed up everything he had to say anyway; and having realised this, he resigned himself to fate and finished off the remains of the concoction, and slid under the table with the others.

Dr Sean Kildare then rose and gave what proved to be a speech with a moral.

'Gentlemen of the Ferret and Firkin Cricket Club . . . and ladies,' he began formally. 'I would like to tell you all that since the formation of our club I have spent some of the happiest moments of my life. I must say that the games I have played with you and the good times I have had with you all have reminded me of an incident which happened to me many years ago when I was a student.

'I had gone to Dublin to see some old friends and on this particular night we had one hell of a session in the lovely

Dublin Tap Rooms. I was staying on the floor of my friend's garret on the top floor of a tenement overlooking a convent.

'Well, in the morning I woke up early with one hell of a head on me and a mouth like the inside of a cabby's glove. As I pulled the curtains the morning light hit me and Jesus it nearly took my head off. But as I focussed on the building opposite, I saw straight away, to my horror, that the window-cleaner was hanging by his fingernails to the window sills of the ninth floor, his ladder having fallen away.

'Well, you can imagine the scream I let out. I tore out of the room and down the stairs shouting for help for the poor man. I burst through the front door and into the street shouting for someone to help him.

'Course, by the time I'd got down there my eyes had become more accustomed to the light and as I stood in the middle of the street in my underpants and vest, having stopped every passerby and the traffic, I looked up and realised that the window-cleaner was in fact, the crucifix stuck on the convent wall.'

Dr Kildare paused as the laughter filled the room and then continued. 'Well, gentlemen, there is a moral to this story which I liken to our club. Sometimes we make absolute prats of ourselves – but it's always with the greatest of intentions.'

'Gentlemen,' he concluded, 'I toast you all.'

After the applause had died down, not to be outdone, Fingers Ashton rose. 'My dear Chaps and Chapesses,' he began, informally, 'I too have a moralistic story, nay, a parable. It concerns my dear grandfather.'

The Tap Room fell quiet in anticipation.

'Many years ago he was playing cricket for a team in Blackpool. He was never a batsman – he hardly knew which end of a bat was which. Now, his side fielded first and bowled the other side out for less than a hundred. Grandad, having bowled particularly well, went back to the pavilion believing that he wouldn't be needed for the rest of the day. And so he settled into his favourite pastime – whisky drinking.

'Well, the other team took to the field and they proved to be a right lot of bastards, bowling plenty of bouncers on a very hard and unpredictable wicket. This was all pre-Bodyline remember, and quite a lot of intended run-out throws ended up hitting the batsmen. Scoring runs was about as difficult as confirming a game over the telephone with the secretary of that deaf team we played.

'Well, pretty soon the side had lost eight of the team, most of them retired hurt. And they had made less than half of the required total.

'Grandad had watched all of these goings-on grumbling and mumbling into his whisky bottle and pretty soon, much to his dislike, it was his turn to bat.

'He put on his one dirty pad and a left-handed glove, he borrowed a bat and then finished the bottle. He strode out to bat through his injured team mates, swearing under his breath.

'When he got to the wicket he didn't even bother to take a guard, he just growled at everyone. He then went on to smash the bowlers all over the place in an angry innings which has become known in my family's folklore as "Ashton's last stand". He managed to pinch the batting each time from his battered partner and went on to score a crushing, violent, indignant 50 and win the game. He left the field, still growling under his breath, the hero of the day.'

Here Fingers paused for breath and took a deep swig of his pint.

'And the moral of this story, lads, is: don't mess around with my Grandad when he's pissed!'

Anyway, Lucky, by this time the rest of the members of the team had more or less succumbed to the quality or quantity of whatever they were drinking. By the time it came to opening time the Tap Room looked like a hospital casualty area – something I'm sure you're familiar with.

There was only one team member who was still sober.

Me.

I sat there taking it all in, my crotch steaming.

I took full advantage of my sober state and borrowed the landlord's camera. The pictures I took are delightful and are now all together in a large frame adorning the Tap Room wall: an assortment of pub cricketers after a heavy season.

Revenge is so sweet.

I must admit that thoughts of blackmail did cross my mind as I was snapping away, especially when I focussed on one particular scene in Crossword Corner. There was Big Al cuddled up with Rayleen. At their feet was Typhoon Turnbull cuddled up with Satan.

At the piano slept Fingers Ashton with Dick Dickinson asleep on top of it.

Under the table were Mr Gloomburg, Romeley, the General and Sean Kildare, all snoring in harmony.

Cronin the Librarian was later found asleep with his head in the pan of the Gents' loo. Apparently he thought he could wake himself up by taking a shower.

Dave the Grave was dozing propped up against the bar, the occasional, 'Nyer . . .' punctuating his heavy breathing.

The lovely Jan staggered up to me and took my arm and smiled that heart-melting smile of hers. 'Nobody's perfect,' she said.

'Thank God,' I replied. I then had the pleasure of escorting her home.

How the others got home that night I don't know.

All the prize-givings – best bowler, batsman, drinker etc. – were done over the following days as plans were being made for us to tour Australia at Christmas. The biggest worry seems to be just how much proper beer we'll be allowed to take with us through customs.

If we do get there I think Mr Gloomburg's concoctions will be more welcome than ever.

So Lucky, dear mate, it has been a momentous year. We have established what I believe to be a major force in the cricketing world: The Tap Room CC.

And God bless all who sail in her.

For now, all the very best from myself and all in the Tap Room.

Cheers and good health,

Steve.